Happy Brain, Happy Life:
Everyday Neuroscience for Health, Wealth, and Love

By Peter Hollins,

Author and Researcher at

petehollins.com

Table of Contents

CHAPTER 1: THE HEALTHY BRAIN

WHAT ARE THE PHYSICAL CHARACTERISTICS OF A HEALTHY BRAIN?
SUNLIGHT AND SEROTONIN
SLEEP HYGIENE AND BRAIN HEALTH
THE BRAIN NEEDS DOWNTIME

CHAPTER 2: THE RESILIENT BRAIN

WHAT STRESS DOES TO YOUR BRAIN
THE SOCIAL BRAIN IS A HAPPY BRAIN
LAUGH IT OFF!
DANCING CAN BOOST SEROTONIN LEVELS

CHAPTER 3: THE STORYTELLING BRAIN

JOURNALING REWIRES THE BRAIN
THE NEUROSCIENCE OF THE READING
WATCH YOUR LANGUAGE!

CHAPTER 4: THE CONNECTED BRAIN

YOUR BRAIN WANTS A PURPOSE
GENEROSITY TRIGGERS THE HAPPINESS TRIFECTA
SELF-COMPASSION IS IMPORTANT, TOO

CHAPTER 5: THE DISCIPLINED BRAIN

LEARNING TO BE OPTIMISTIC
TO MASTER YOUR FEELINGS, LEARN TO PUT THEM INTO WORDS
GOAL SETTING TRIGGERS DOPAMINE

CHAPTER 6: THE AGILE BRAIN

THE SPICE OF LIFE
CREATIVITY AND BRAIN HEALTH
MINDSET: THINK GROWTH, CREATE GROWTH
FOR THE BRAIN, CURIOSITY EQUALS REWARD

Chapter 1: The Healthy Brain

We'll begin this book with a question: What is the **mind** and what is the **brain**? And what is their relationship to one another?

Definitions sometimes tell us that "the mind is what perceives, reasons, remembers, imagines, etc." and that the mind encompasses "conscious and unconscious processes and mental phenomena." The mind, we are told, is the seat of consciousness and the thing we use to think and feel and perceive.

Although this tells us what the mind does, it doesn't really tell us what the mind is. Thought, memory, learning, imagination, consciousness, perception, mood, and motivation are very different activities . . . yet we attribute them all to the mind. If those activities stop, then where is the mind?

The brain is easier to define: It's that organ that sits inside your skull.

What, then, is the relationship between brain and mind?

Consider that a human being is like an instrument, say a violin. There is the violin itself—the body, the neck, the strings, the bow—but there is also the potential for music, which is what the violin has been made for. In this metaphor, the brain is the physical violin, and the music it creates is the mind. Brain and mind are two aspects of the same thing, but the brain **is**, while the mind **does**.

In much the same way as a violinist can master their craft by learning all about music and its creation, they won't get very far if the physical instrument itself is damaged. If a violin's strings are out of tune, the bow too loose, or the body chipped and broken, then the violin won't play properly no matter how skilled the violinist!

The psychological approach to self-improvement focuses on the mind, i.e., the experiences and outward manifestations of the activity of the brain. In this book, however, we'll be focusing on the other side of the equation: the brain itself.

We'll be paying close attention to the *physiological aspects* of our psychological well-being, because it's only when the brain itself is happy and healthy that the mind can be healthy. When the brain as an organ is strong, healthy, and resilient, then the mind reflects this in the form of flexibility, creativity, resilience, and so on. Just as good music is a natural expression of a well-maintained violin, a healthy mind is the natural expression of a healthy brain.

What Are the Physical Characteristics of a Healthy Brain?

Have you ever thought about the physical condition of your brain?

For the vast majority of us, our brain is something secret and invisible, and if we're lucky, we are born and we die never setting eyes on it. Perhaps we forget that it's there at all and don't appreciate that it's composed of living tissues and blood vessels, just like the other limbs and organs of the body.

Your arms, legs, hands, feet, facial features . . . all of these things are uniquely yours and change according to their state of health. The same is true of your brain, which is just as unique as the rest of you, and the health of which is just as dependent on its environment.

Before we can understand how to achieve a healthy brain, we need to understand exactly what a healthy brain is. A healthy heart is strong and pink, a healthy digestive tract is smooth and muscular, and healthy skin is supple and thick. What does a healthy brain look like?

Take a look at the image below. It comes from a paper by Pallawi and Singh (2023), published in the *International Journal of Multimedia Retrieval.*

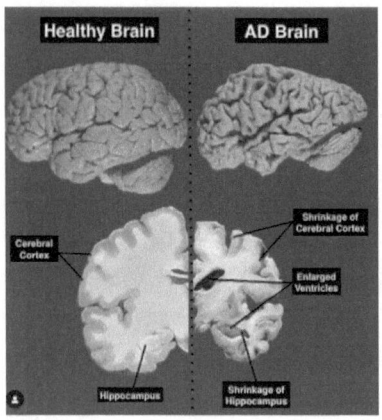

The image makes it very clear what a healthy brain is *not*; on the right we see a brain ravaged by Alzheimer's disease. The ventricles (spaces or gaps) are much bigger, the hippocampus and cortex are both smaller, and the total brain volume is noticeably decreased. The brain on the right can be considered to have undergone rapid aging and deterioration.

There is good reason to believe that brain volume is directly correlated with overall brain health and function. One study by UC Davis Health researchers has found that human brains are actually increasing in average size over time, with people in the 1970s possessing brains 6.6 percent larger in volume and 15 percent greater in surface area than people born in the 1930s.

So, although the population in the US is aging, the incidence of Alzheimer's (i.e., the proportion of the population affected) is actually decreasing. Researchers believe that one of the reasons is the increase in brain volume, which may act as a "reserve" that offsets the shrinking we see in the image above.

"Larger brain structures like those observed in our study may reflect improved brain development and improved brain health. A larger brain structure represents a larger brain reserve and may buffer the late-life effects of age-related brain diseases like Alzheimer's and related dementias," claims author Charles DeCarli (2024).

This "brain reserve hypothesis" suggests that bigger brains may reduce dementia risk, primarily because of the implications for the way the brain can function. It's not just the fact of size, of course, but what the increased volume represents: Larger brains mean more neurons and more synaptic connections between those neurons.

Okay, so a healthy brain is a BIG brain. What else?

Take a look at another set of interesting brain scans:

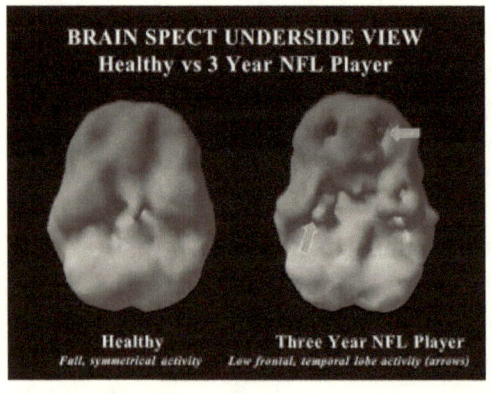

The above are SPECT brain scans indicating the impaired blood flow in an NFL player compared to someone with a healthy brain (from the University of California Los Angeles

Medical Center). A SPECT scan is a kind of brain imaging technique that uses radioactive substances to create useful images of the body, often the brain or heart. They can be used in particular to show how well blood manages to flow through a certain area, and subsequently how active and healthy that area is.

Cerebral circulation refers to the blood flow to the brain, and without it, the brain is at risk of stroke, hypoxia, hemorrhage, and edema. Low blood flow does not have to be that severe to create problems, however. Blood carries oxygen and nutrients to the brain and carries waste materials away, so any disturbance to this flow will naturally interfere with good brain function. In fact, to achieve its important work of keeping the brain continuously nourished and oxygenated, the brain demands a full 15 percent of the heart's total cardiac output, which is enormous considering its small size compared to the rest of the body.

Cerebral circulation is not all that matters when it comes to brain health, but it is certainly an indication of activity and vitality. The scans above clearly reveal reduced blood flow to the NFL player's brain, which can spell serious brain damage. SPECT scans have also revealed a similar reduction of blood flow in those who abuse alcohol or drugs, or even those who chronically under-sleep. We can conclude, then, that a healthy brain is one that receives rich, ample blood flow.

Finally, let's zoom in a little and look at the brain in terms of its neurotransmitters, using the helpful acronym DOSE. Current neuroscience research is unanimous in its conclusion that a healthy brain is one that is producing optimal levels of the most important neurotransmitters:

Dopamine

Oxytocin

Serotonin

Endorphins

The Recipe for a Healthy Brain

If we want to start building a healthy brain, then we need to know the basic parameters we're aiming for: A healthy brain is large and has a large surface area, is smooth and pink (indicating a good blood flow to and from the brain), and has small ventricles. Up close, it is rich in neurons (brain cells) that are well-connected to one another. Finally, a healthy brain has optimal levels of DOSE neurotransmitters. Let's briefly consider each of these neurotransmitters in terms of their function.

Dopamine

This neurotransmitter regulates and modulates the "reward system" in the brain. It's associated with pleasure, motivation, and drive and produces good feelings when you're reaching for or achieving a new goal, or else completing a challenging task.

Too much dopamine may leave a person acting aggressively or impulsively. Too little and they may experience apathy and a lack of motivation. Low levels are also connected with depression, psychosis, and even schizophrenia, although the relationship may be bidirectional, meaning low levels of dopamine and mental illness often mutually cause one another. Dysregulated dopamine levels have long been associated with addictions of all kinds, as well as with the mechanisms behind ADHD.

Dopamine is not just about the *feeling* of motivation and reward; it also has pronounced physical effects such as the regulation of sleep, sex drive, muscle health, and digestion. Dopamine function is extremely complex and not merely a matter of levels that are either too high or low. What's more, contrary to popular advice out there, it is neither possible nor desirable to "detox" from dopamine. Rather, dopamine can be understood as a key player in a complicated symphony of motivation, anticipation, arousal, and reward—what matters is timing and its relative interactions with other neurotransmitters.

Oxytocin

Oxytocin is often called the "love hormone" and is associated with feelings of warmth, liking, trust, and closeness. Its role is the creation and maintenance of social relationships, since it creates feelings of security and calm contentment with others. Oxytocin plays a role in human reproduction (such as in sex, childbirth, and lactation) and is triggered in response to human touch, massage, music, exercise, cuddling, or even stroking a pet.

Just like with dopamine, however, it's a question of optimal levels—overly high oxytocin has been associated with prostate enlargement in men and too-strong contractions during labor. Too little oxytocin may mean weak labor contractions, sexual difficulties, insomnia, and sleep trouble.

Serotonin

The "happiness hormone" is all about feeling valued and has links to the social experience of status and recognition. Serotonin is linked with confidence and feelings of efficacy and well-being, which in turn enables people to create social harmony, adapt to challenges, and solve problems.

Low serotonin levels are found in people who are depressed, anxious, or unable to sleep properly, and a serotonin deficit often correlates with things like irritability and difficulty reaching orgasm. Too much serotonin, on the other hand, can lead to confusion, seizures, and shivering, or so-called serotonin syndrome, which can be a dangerous side effect of SSRIs (selective serotonin reuptake inhibitors) (Bakshi and Tadi 2022).

Endorphins

You may have heard about endorphins as the neurotransmitters responsible for "runner's high." The term comes from "*endo*genous mor*phine*" because these chemicals act like the body's own (endogenous) painkillers (like morphine), creating a brief euphoria that offsets the experience of physical pain . . . such as when you've been running for too long and your knees start to hurt!

Endorphins are usually released in response to any physical stress, pain, or exertion. Low endorphin levels have been linked to depression, anxiety, sleep problems, substance abuse, migraines, mood swings, and even muscular aches and pains. Endorphin levels rise and fall throughout the day, and they help regulate your sense of self-esteem, your appetite, and your immune system, in concert with all the other neurotransmitters.

Endorphins also increase during pleasurable activities like exercise, sleeping, eating, and sex. Higher levels may feel good, but they may also make some people chase the feeling a little too obsessively, creating unhealthy habitual behaviors such as exercise addiction, thrill-seeking, or even self-harm (Chaudhry and Gossman 2023).

In the "recipe for a healthy brain," we can imagine that these four neurotransmitters (as well as many others) combine to create sophisticated brain states that influence our experience in subtle and profound ways. Rather than trying to tweak each level separately, however, we can instead see our goal as the creation of an external environment that best supports our brain's innate ability to balance and regulate itself. By creating the optimal conditions, we allow our brain to find its own natural and healthy equilibrium.

In the rest of our book, we'll be exploring the many ways to support our brain health, especially as it's manifested through the activity of the neurotransmitters. The good news is that the brain is a part of the body, and that means that everything that is healthy for the body in general is also healthy for the brain:

- Consistent, good quality sleep and rest
- Adequate hydration
- Manageable stress levels
- Physical exercise
- Fresh air
- A happy, meaningful, and integrated social life
- Challenging work, achievable goals, and a purpose
- Joy, pleasure, and fun
- Reducing harmful elements like alcohol, processed food, drug use, or chronic stress

So, to conclude, what are the physical characteristics of a healthy brain? We can say that a happy brain is large, well-connected, and with healthy blood flow and optimal and balanced levels of neurotransmitters. Now, unless you have brain scan gadgets in your home or supernatural abilities, chances are you won't get to peek inside your own skull anytime soon, and you won't easily know how healthy your brain is given these metrics.

What you *can* do, however, is consult the best research evidence and make educated decisions about your lifestyle so you can give your brain the best chance at health and vitality. You can also pay close attention to the quality of your *mind* and make inferences about the health of your brain, remembering that the way we think, feel, and perceive is directly connected to the physical health and functioning of our brain. For example, if you consistently find yourself feeling unconfident, anxious, or undervalued, you may become curious about the way serotonin is functioning for you, and start to take steps known to support ideal serotonin balance in the brain. In fact, this is the theme for our next section.

Sunlight and Serotonin

Andrew Humington is the founder of *Neuromastery* and the author of *The Neuroscience of Morning Routines: How to Increase Dopamine and Motivation*. According to him, "what happens to you in the hour after you wake up primes your brain for the rest of the day . . . for better or worse!"

We've all experienced those fantastic mornings where we feel energized and focused and zoom through our tasks with zest and clarity. And then there are some mornings where we feel sloppy, unorganized, and grumpy and can't seem to do anything we set our minds to . . .

The thing making all the difference? It may be the sunshine. Humington claims that sunlight shining directly into your eyes within the first hour of waking doesn't just feel good—it genuinely *is* good for your health and well-being. Human circadian rhythms have evolved over thousands of years, and our wake/sleep biology is tightly modulated by the signals received from the environment. Natural sunlight regulates cortisol levels, boosts alertness and focus, and balances mood.

Neuroscientist and professor Andrew Huberman agrees and also advises people to not just seek out sunlight in the mornings, but throughout the day. In his popular podcast, Huberman Labs, he points out the many surprising impacts of natural light on the human body.

"Light directly impacts our mood, our sleep, our ability to wake up and focus, our hormone levels, our immune system, and our ability to cope with stress," he claims. "I consider viewing morning sunlight in the top five of all actions (along with sleep, movement, nutrient intake, and relationships) that support mental health, physical health, and performance."

The daily flow of light and darkness is a powerful regulator of our hormones and coordinates the release of many important substances in the body, serotonin and melatonin in particular. While sunlight triggers the release of serotonin (which leads to enhanced mood, calm, and focus), darkness triggers melatonin release (which leads to the body's preparations for sleep).

As you can imagine, dysregulation in these two chemicals can leave you feeling groggy and unfocused during the day, or else suffering insomnia at night, when you should be sleeping. Simply imagine that serotonin enables a state of general wakefulness in your brain and that the sun acts as a kind of switch for that serotonin release.

It's not just wakefulness, either, but also mood. Researchers for the National Institute of Mental Health (NIMH), led by Samer Hattar, found a direct correlation between sunlight levels and the experience of SAD (seasonal adjustment disorder), a condition characterized by low mood during the winter months.

In the past, researchers believed that the eye contained only two kinds of cells—rods and cones. A third photoreceptor has been identified, however, and these are called intrinsically photosensitive retinal ganglion cells, or ipRGCs. Their job is to receive and perceive light, but they are not part of the ordinary image-creation machinery of the rest of the eye. Instead, they contain melanopsin, which is a light-sensitive protein not found in the other photoreceptors.

The ipRGCs help regulate the body's biological clock (circadian rhythm) and keep us matched up to the twenty-four-hour diurnal cycle. Researchers discovered that when sunlight reaches the ipRGCs, this stimulates a pathway through the brain and into the ventromedial prefrontal cortex—a part of the brain closely connected with reward, mood, and decision-making.

In other words, there is a *direct physiological link* between the sunlight you see in the morning and the feeling of well-being and purpose you bring to the rest of the day. You don't need a neuroscience degree to understand that it's a good idea to maximize sunlight exposure!

Here are a few of Huberman's tips for getting the most of the sunshine (even if it's winter or you don't live in a sunny place!):

1. **Gaze in the general direction of the sun without actually staring at it—** which is obviously damaging for your eyes. Staring at any bright light for too long, natural or artificial, can create eye tension. Instead, just imagine that you're a sunflower and gently facing the sun without looking squarely at it.
2. Contacts and eyeglasses, even those with UV protection, won't interfere with your morning sunlight viewing, and they won't affect the stimulation of the ipRGCs. Try to **avoid sunglasses**, however, since these may actively prevent certain wavelengths from entering the retina.
3. **Aim for a minimum of five to ten minutes** of sunlight on sunny days and fifteen to twenty minutes on grayer days. You don't have to sit there motionless; try having a walk, drinking your coffee, having breakfast, journaling, or engaging in pleasant conversation while in the sunshine. A daily routine of this kind will provide stability and consistency to your sleep habits.

4. **Don't worry about cloudy days.** You can still achieve some benefit by merely sitting by a bright enough window. If it's a truly dark and cloudy day, don't worry: You can still experience the regulating effects of the sun by being outside as much as possible. Combined with physical exercise and fresh air (which can also boost serotonin levels), this common-sense treatment for SAD may be the most effective yet.

5. **If the sun is extremely bright and strong, use SPF to protect your skin.** Receiving sunlight directly onto the skin of your body is valuable, too, but weigh up the benefits against the risks of exposing yourself to burns.

If you have been battling anxiety, depression, irritability, low self-confidence, or poor sleep (i.e., all signs of low serotonin levels), then consider implementing this easy but very effective trick. A great idea is to make a habit of it: When you wake up in the morning, immediately get up and out of bed, open the curtains, open the windows, and draw a good few lungfuls of fresh air. Speaking of waking up, let's now move on to another easy but very effective way to boost brain health: good sleep.

Sleep Hygiene and Brain Health

Sleep is important for the brain because it represents its principal method for rejuvenation. The brain is a metabolically active organ that gets tired just like every other part of you ... and throughout the course of the day, metabolites and toxins build up in the brain tissues. Sleep is the time your brain gets to clear away this debris and flush out harmful substances so that, on waking, you are ready to freshly seize the day again.

There is a little gap around each brain cell called the interstitial space, and during sleep this space expands, allowing your brain to initiate a kind of "clean up and repair" program all around it.

"The restorative function of sleep may be due to the switching of the brain into a state that facilitates the clearance of waste products that accumulate during wakefulness," says Dr. Rashid Deane, neuromedicine professor at the University of Rochester Medical Center. The brain, unlike other organs in the body, isn't linked up to the body's lymphatic system, which would normally clear away accumulated toxins. Instead, the cerebrospinal fluid continuously cycles throughout the brain, and during sleep, once the interstitial spaces have expanded, it can transfer toxins over to be flushed away.

You can think of this process as a little like someone cleaning up their house after they've just hosted a party. There's no point cleaning up while the guests are still there and having a good time, and besides, the host is needed to take care of their guests and socialize. Only when the party's over and everyone has gone home does the host get to work tidying up. Your brain is the same. It cannot initiate the clean-up program while it's still doing the work of the day. It's only during sleep that it switches roles. The day is for spending your cognitive budget; the night is for earning it back.

If you've ever had a very poor night's sleep, you'll already be well aware of just how much your brain needs this clean up and repair routine, and how quickly you can fall behind without it. Even one night of poor-quality sleep can leave you feeling groggy, unrefreshed, and unable to concentrate or think clearly. Interestingly, one of the materials cleared away during sleep is called beta-amyloid, and its buildup is associated with the development of dementia conditions like Alzheimer's.

One study linked sleep deprivation with the development of harmful amyloid plaques

(2012). Dr. Adam Spira, the research lead, claims that,

> "For a long time, scientists believed that people with dementia don't sleep well because their brains are adversely affected by neurodegenerative disease. But within the last 10 years or so, researchers have begun pondering whether insomnia might also be a potential cause of cognitive decline rather than simply something that emerges as a result of a neurodegenerative disease."

In other words, dementia may be a symptom of sleep deprivation, and not the other way around! Don't panic about having a few poor nights here and there, however—this is unlikely to bring on dementia, and the correlations between sleep and cognitive impairment are multifactorial and still being investigated. However, the results are clear: Sleep is extremely important.

The Golden Rules of Good Sleep

Sleep is a strange lifestyle habit. Many of us simply assume that a good night's sleep is natural and automatic—and not something you can necessarily be "good" at. But even though sleep is a normal and healthy part of life, it does sometimes take deliberate effort to practice good sleep habits. The first thing is to realize that your current routine may not in fact be working for you, even if you've done it for years!

Though the tips below may seem a little basic, their value becomes evident when they're most consistently applied. If making changes to your sleep is not something you've really done before, a good first step is just to monitor your present situation for a week or two. This is because self-reports of sleep quantity and quality are often distorted, i.e., we are usually poor judges of the quality of our own sleep.

Keep a log of daily bedtimes and wake times and rate your feeling of refreshment upon waking each morning, as well as how alert and energized you felt during the day when you go to bed. Keep track of things that may be influencing your sleep, like alcohol intake, stress, irregular work patterns, and the like. Then, look for patterns—you may be surprised at what you find when you deliberately monitor yourself.

Once you have a good idea of where you may be falling short, consider gradually implementing some of these golden rules:

Keep it consistent. Go to bed at the same time each night and wake up at the same time each morning. There's no point in trying to "bank" sleep on the weekend to counterbalance late nights during the week, for example. It's not just the number of total hours that counts—the consistent routine matters more.

Have a bedtime routine. Try not to dive straight into bed, but rather ease into sleep by having a buffer period where you slowly unwind and relax. Rituals prime your brain, cement good habits, and prepare you for better quality rest. Good rituals include any soothing activities you like, such as a warm bath, light reading, snuggling, or meditating. Avoid heavy conversations, exercise, and big meals, and try to reserve your bed for sleeping only, or sex; avoid using your bed as a place to watch TV, eat, study, or browse social media, since you'll be teaching your brain to associate your bed with activity rather than rest.

Banish electronics and screens. Your bedroom should be a haven away from blinking lights and glowing screens. Keep TVs, digital clocks, laptops, and other devices out, and make sure that no bright LED lights are blinking in the darkness. You might like to keep your phone next to your bed in case of emergency, but if so, keep it on silent and put it inside a drawer where you cannot see or hear it.

Have a caffeine cut-off. Whether you drink tea, coffee, or soda, have a cut-off time beyond which you won't drink any more caffeine-containing beverages. Even chocolate can aggravate caffeine-sensitive people, so try to avoid anything potentially triggering after 3 p.m. or so. You may also choose to cut down on liquids in general to avoid having to wake at night to use the bathroom. Finally, alcohol can seriously worsen sleep quality, so try to cut back as much as possible.

Keep it dark. Remembering that darkness stimulates melatonin release, do what you can to shut out bright light. Use black-out curtains or shutters or find a good sleep mask. If you wake up to use the bathroom at night, consider going in the dark or using a very gentle nightlight that won't disrupt your night's sleep too much.

Pay attention to bedding. Do a "bedroom audit" where you check up on the quality of your mattress and pillows—poor support during sleep can create a host of health problems and interfere with your circulation, not to mention leave you feeling cranky and unrefreshed. Always make sure you have fresh, clean bedding (preferably in natural or breathable materials) and sleepwear that is comfortable and non-restrictive.

Address sleep conditions. Are you a snorer? Or do you have to sleep next to one? Sleep apnea and snoring can be incredibly disruptive and should ideally be treated by a doctor, as should conditions like teeth grinding or night sweats, which may indicate menopause, thyroid problems, or autoimmune conditions.

One great piece of advice comes from Dr. Jess Andrade, who popularized her "10-3-2-1-0 method" on social media. It's a simple rule of thumb that helps you gradually count down to bedtime:

- **10** hours before bed: Stay away from certain drinks (coffee, tea) to give your body enough time to flush the caffeine from your system.
- **3** hours before bed: This should be the time of your last meal, and preferably it should not be a heavy one. This reduces strain on your digestive system and prevents things like reflux or even nightmares.
- **2** hours before bed: Deliberately start relaxing and unwinding. Essentially, start allowing your brain to unplug! A mental break will help you fall off to sleep more easily and improve the quality of rest once you're asleep.

- **1 hour before bed:** Make this the cut-off for screen time. Blue light can be hazardous for sleep since it resembles morning light and triggers wakefulness, confusing both your body and brain.
- **0**: In the morning, when you wake up—fully wake up! Don't hit the snooze button and don't linger around in bed for too long. Instead, get up, move, breathe deeply, and find yourself some natural light. This will help you start the day refreshed and ready to go. Interestingly, one of the best predictors for a good night's sleep may be the quality of the morning that came before it . . . so set the stage right and give yourself the best chance for deep, truly restorative sleep.

If sleep is an issue for you, it may be that you've gotten stuck in a vicious cycle. A study done by Simon et al. (2020) showed that sleep deprivation can negatively affect the medial prefrontal cortex. Because this part of the brain is involved in anxiety management, a lack of sleep can leave you feeling less able to manage stress, regulate your emotions, and deal with everyday problems and irritations. At the same time, sleep deprivation can lead to overactivity in the amygdala, which correlates with emotional instability and stress.

The trouble is that if you're already irritable, emotional, and stressed, you are less likely to take steps that support your good health. Feeling strung out from a hard day, you may decide to "treat" yourself to a late night, spend too much time doomscrolling or watching TV, drink too much, overeat, or otherwise engage in habits that destroy your sleep quality . . . and the cycle continues.

This is why it's worth being patient when you make changes to your sleep routine. It may feel a little uncomfortable at first, but soon the changes will start to feel more natural, and the vicious cycle will be reversed. Eventually, you will find it much easier and more enjoyable to have healthy sleep habits.

The Brain Needs Downtime

Occasionally, a productivity guru or self-help influencer will share their idealized daily routine. They'll show an impressive daily schedule that includes eight hours of perfect sleep, plenty of exercise, big chunks of effective work, and a string of other beneficial activities crammed in between. Conspicuously absent from these minutely programmed schedules is one unappreciated part of a healthy life: rest.

Sleep is essential, of course—but sleep is not the same as rest, and the brain and body need sleep *and* rest.

Unfortunately, our productivity-obsessed culture can make us uncomfortable with the idea of big empty gaps in our calendars where we're "not doing anything." We'd prefer that everything be productive, even our nonproductivity! So, we treat even rest and contemplation as just one more stressful item on the to-do list: meditate for ten minutes, then journal and find something to be grateful for, then do a breathing exercise (perfectly), then look at nature for fifteen minutes, then get back to work . . .

Julia Kocian is a social worker and mental health counselor and claims that "many people don't often have a choice in how much rest is available to them. The way society is set up, we treat rest as a privilege, not a right."

The "politics of rest" is unfortunately complicated, but beyond making the societal and economic changes necessary to completely reframe our attitudes and assumptions around rest, we can do a lot to deliberately incorporate more health-giving rest into our own lives.

When you rest, your brain is no longer active, which means its energies and efforts can go elsewhere, namely to consolidating what has already transpired in the more active parts of your day. Like everything in nature, your brain's alertness and strength rises and falls in cycles, with rest enabling and supporting action.

Too many people have the attitude that rest is a kind of defeat, a sign of weakness, an indulgence, a rare and unfortunate lapse, a treat or reward, or perhaps even a sign that something is wrong. Negative attitudes like these can make us feel that rest is simply *doing nothing*, or a mere absence of something with real value.

The truth is, rest is not nothing; it's a little like the moments of silence between the notes in music, or the empty space between each word printed on a page. These gaps are not "nothing," and they serve as important a function as the notes and the words. You can't have music without silence, or writing without white space. Similarly, you cannot have active thinking, creativity, problem-solving, emotion, and perception without the brain's own version of "empty space"—that is, rest, contemplation, relaxation, and open-ended daydreaming.

How often have you struggled over a problem only to find that the answer occurred to you at some random moment when you weren't even thinking about it? How often have you woken up with a fresh, useful idea in your mind, all without your conscious effort to create it?

Taking Breaks Is an Art Form

There are better and worse ways to take breaks. Some less-than-ideal ways include:

- Working yourself to death and stopping only because you literally can't go on
- "Taking a break" while anxiously ruminating about the things you're not doing or the things you will do once your break is over
- Taking breaks that you think you *should* find relaxing, even though you really don't
- Relegating breaks to the leftover bits of time in your schedule, or treating breaks as the lowest priority to be scheduled only "if you get around to it"
- Counting sleep as rest

The "goal"—if we can risk saying that there is one—is to completely relax your nervous system and disengage from conscious, active mental effort. Luckily, this broad definition leaves you plenty of room to rest in a way that works for you. If meditation is boring and irritating, then give it a skip. If you find yourself truly "unplugging" when you go for a walk or do a strenuous workout, then do that. For some people, a few hours spent chatting over nothing with friends is the most deeply restorative activity they can imagine (depending, of course, on who the friends are!).

What calms and rebalances one person may actively stress out and annoy another, so don't be afraid to experiment a little. It may be that context and timing matters—for example, you find cooking relaxing and restful when you're doing it on holiday, but stressful on busy weeknights.

The idea is to simply stop and let go. Shift from *doing* mode and into *being* mode.

This means that you may need to refrain from planning what you do during rest periods at all. Simply allow yourself to be a little directionless for a moment. Don't take any further information in, don't process anything, don't respond and react. Just be with yourself in the moment and settle.

Kocian further explains,

> "It's not inherently bad that we want to set goals and achieve them—this helps us contribute to work and home environments and use our time in a way that gives us meaning. But the idea that

we have to constantly be doing something is born from there, and it can make it hard to pause for rest."

Sometimes the biggest obstacle to our own deep rest is not the demands of our job or other people's expectations, but our own beliefs and assumptions about value, effort, and what a good life "should" look like.

It's no wonder that rest and self-compassion go hand in hand—if we can give ourselves permission to just be without earning our sense of worth through action and production, then we may find it easier to take care of ourselves, respect our limits, and find value in who we are outside of what we do.

There is no need (and indeed no way) to maximize rest, or to do it competitively. Nobody is watching and scoring you, and you don't need to compare yourself to anyone else. The irony is that, when we return to a more active mode after resting, we often feel ourselves to be more focused, stronger, more creative, and more energetic. The big insight, of course, is that rest never undermines or takes away from our productivity—it is what allows our productivity.

Victoria Garfield is a senior research fellow at the Medical Research Council Unit for Lifelong Health and Aging, and she and her team published a study in the journal *Sleep Health*. The study analyzed data from more than thirty-five thousand adults and found that people who made a habit of daytime napping tended to have greater brain volume. In fact, they found that there was an average volume increase of fifteen cubic centimeters—an amount her team estimated correlated with 2.5–6.5 years of life.

"Quite a big thing in terms of the age of the brain," said Garfield. "And we think that's really important because a lower total brain volume is linked to certain diseases, earlier mortality and higher stress levels" (2023).

A 2007 study by Richard Chambers found that people who took on a meditating habit actually showed performance improvements on cognitive tests, and another study showed that as little as twelve minutes a day of meditation helped improve the working memories of US Marines (Jha 2011). Meditation breaks increase brain volume, thicken the prefrontal cortex, and improve the density of the hippocampus, which is essential for the functioning of the memory.

Rest, no matter the form it takes, allows the brain to stop and find its balance again. Neurotransmitter levels stabilize, stress and tension drop, and the brain disengages.

Luckily, resting is the easiest thing in the world—we just have to get out of our own way long enough to do it.

A few ideas for gently shifting your attitude around rest:

- Notice when you start to think of busyness as a badge of honor and instead start to see value in having the wisdom to take care of and regulate yourself.
- Scheduling breaks is great because you're telling yourself that you value your downtime. You can also learn to notice your own signs of fatigue, however, and build in multiple "mini breaks" all throughout the day. These can last just a few minutes, yet drastically change your outlook and functioning.
- Social media scrolling and reading the news are **not** restful activities since they actually stimulate information processing (and likely stir up emotional arousal, too).
- Get into the habit of doing a quick "body scan" where you pause to take stock of your energy and attention levels. Notice your breathing, muscle tension, mood, posture, and ability to concentrate. If you're feeling fatigued and losing focus,

consciously choose to pause and come back later when you're more refreshed.
- Set the stage. Going into nature is restful, but so is enjoying special places you've set aside simply to chill out in. Tune out distractions, leave screens and phones behind, and take yourself off the clock. You may find it easier to rest and replenish when you're in a comfortable, private, and beautiful setting.
- Sometimes, simply stepping away from an intense activity is enough to help your brain disconnect and start to consolidate. Go for a short, brisk walk, change tack and do some cleaning or other household chores, have a shower, or simply get up and stretch or move around.
- Protect your rest time from others who would encroach on it. Politely but firmly assert your limits, and don't let guilt or obligation make you feel that you owe other people your productivity.

Summary:

- The mind is the expression of the activity of the brain; only when the brain is healthy can the mind be healthy.

- The physical characteristics of a healthy brain include large volume, small gaps and spaces, well-connected neurons, and good blood supply. A healthy brain also has optimal levels of the important "DOSE" neurotransmitter—dopamine, oxytocin, serotonin, and endorphins. Each of these serves a particular set of complicated and interconnected functions in the brain.
- A few minutes of indirect sunlight in the morning can regulate serotonin levels, boost mood, and help you maintain focus and energy for the rest of the day.
- Good sleep is essential since it helps the brain recuperate, rest, and repair, as well as flush out accumulated toxins from the day. Keep a consistent routine and practice good sleep hygiene to keep your brain functioning optimally.
- Finally, your brain needs enough unscheduled, goal-less, and open-ended time for rest, contemplation, and reflection. The brain's alertness and strength rises and falls in cycles, and frequent breaks are necessary to maintain well-being and true productivity. Try to reframe any unhealthy beliefs around downtime—rest is not "doing nothing."

- Completely relax your nervous system and disengage from conscious, active mental effort, and shift from *doing* into *being*—in a way that works for you.

Chapter 2: The Resilient Brain

A healthy brain is one that needs to be able to resist many of life's unfortunate threats and hazards, and if injury *is* sustained, the brain should be able to recover as quickly as possible. In other words, a healthy brain is resilient. So far, we've mentioned a few rather scary things that can happen to the human brain in the course of its lifetime—Alzheimer's disease, brain damage, sleep deprivation, and the ravages of drug and alcohol use to name just a few.

The shocking fact, however, is that the biggest threat to our brain health is not unexpected head injuries or dementia, but rather from a more pervasive, everyday danger: *chronic stress.*

What Stress Does to Your Brain

Stress is everywhere. It's a part of life, and most of us will have to deal with various levels of stress all throughout our lives. But if stress is everywhere, so is resilience and coping. In this section we'll consider the quite serious effects of prolonged stress on the brain, but also take a look at the good news: how to manage it and even, if we're lucky, thrive in it.

First, let's define exactly what we're talking about. Stress can be understood as the body's reaction to challenges and demands in the environment. This is important: Stress is not in your world; it's in your brain. The stress reaction is part of our biological mechanisms for survival; stress forms part of that complicated response that helps us focus on and protect ourselves against threats.

When the body is stressed, it floods with a cascade of hormones (adrenaline, cortisol) that in turn trigger the release of a host of other hormones. The point of this response is to mobilize action that will keep you safe. For example, you may be walking in the woods and your sense organs (eyes and ears) tell you that a wolf is nearby. This perception triggers a series of responses that prime you to act to save yourself—increased heart rate, decreased digestion, pupil dilation, hyperfocus. When the danger passes and the wolf moves on, your body returns to baseline and relaxes again.

This finely tuned evolutionary mechanism doesn't always help us when it comes to the stressors of the modern world, however. Dwelling on money trouble, ruminating over social aggravations, getting stuck in traffic, or worrying about climate change are all stimuli that may be perceived in just the same way as a wolf in the forest . . . except the "danger" might never sufficiently pass, and the body remains in a chronic, prolonged state of hyperarousal that never abates.

A fight-or-flight response is triggered when the HPA axis—which includes the hypothalamus, the pituitary, and the adrenal system—is activated. They orchestrate the release of hormones throughout the body that then stimulate the nervous system. The entire organism undergoes changes—for example, digestion stops, muscles tighten, and heart rate increases. The mind takes on a "tunnel vision" quality and focuses with heightened awareness on the perceived threat, excluding everything else from awareness.

Bruce McEwan is a neuroscientist from Rockefeller University, and he claims that,

> "Because stress changes the way the brain's neurons communicate with

> each other, chronic stress can cause our brains, nervous systems, and our behavior to adjust to a vigilant and reactive state."

Taken to the extreme, this state of hypervigilance can be observed in PTSD and has even been known to affect gene expression across generations. The narrowing of awareness that comes with this kind of hyperfocus means that the brain is constantly giving preferential attention to only those things it perceives as a danger—you can imagine the profound effects of this on a person's worldview over the course of years.

Chronic stress damages the entire body, and it can wreak particular havoc on the brain, leading to long-term inflammation, headaches, memory impairment, disturbed mood, irritability, loss of concentration, and more. If you are constantly stressed, you may tighten your neck muscles and never release them, leading to spasms and pain over time. If you constantly tense your brain and mind in the same way, similar problems occur: cognitive overload, overwhelm, and a loss of ability to focus.

Again, it may be a question of a vicious cycle: For example, we worry about an important upcoming decision and stress about the outcome, but because we do, we put ourselves into a prolonged state of strain, fatiguing our brain so that over time, we genuinely do lose cognitive ability and, ironically, make that poor decision we were so worried about making ... which starts us off stressing again!

Other evidence of a chronically stressed-out brain includes:

- Depression or mood swings
- Anxiety, nervousness, feeling "burned out"
- Feelings of overwhelm
- Irritation and cynicism
- Procrastination
- Brain fog and trouble paying attention
- Worry and rumination, obsessive thinking, intrusive thoughts
- Memory problems
- Nightmares

A *little* stress for a *little* while can be a good thing—it helps you pay attention, get out of danger, and mobilize yourself so that you can rise to challenging tasks. A lot of stress for a long time, however, can be fatal and can reduce your ability to respond to life's challenges in the long term.

Keeping Stress at Bay

The goal is not to have a perfect, easy life with zero challenge or adversity. Rather, the idea is to take advantage of your brain's inbuilt ability for change and growth (that is, its neuroplasticity) and deliberately cultivate your own resilience and coping. We have several ways to reduce the harmful effects of stress on our bodies and minds:

1. Take realistic and active steps to reduce stress triggers in everyday life
2. Build self-awareness so that we know when we are becoming stressed and exactly how to relieve and manage that stress
3. Live well despite the inevitable tensions and discomforts of life—i.e., become mentally tough and resilient

For example, if you notice that work stress is beginning to take its toll on your health, you can tackle the problem from these three perspectives. First, do what can be done to reduce unreasonable workloads and manage expectations on you. This may mean better boundaries and communication with your boss. It may also mean paying better attention to diet, exercise, or other lifestyle habits.

Second, you can try to build more awareness about how you're feeling and how stress shows up in your body, then take time every single day to release that tension—for example, through yoga, guided visualizations, or fun leisure activities that help you take your mind off things.

Finally, you can remind yourself that you are in fact capable of enduring occasional stress because you are strong and can cope. You may use affirmations or certain ways of reframing your thinking to remind yourself that you have survived in the past and will continue to survive now.

These three approaches overlap with one another in real life. Setting better boundaries may in fact boost your feeling of mastery and control, for example, and taking better care of your diet, sleep, and exercise may mean you are better able to really believe in your coping affirmations and trust in your own resilience.

One way to consistently stay on top of stress in your life is to have a regular stress management ritual. Don't wait for life to get out of control or for feelings of overwhelm to stress you—by that point, it may be far too late! Instead, make sure that you're acknowledging and releasing stress each and every day . . . or multiple times a day, if possible.

An effective stress management ritual can be whatever you want, but it does need to be realistically achievable every day, and it should genuinely help you relieve tension and feel calmer and more relaxed. Some examples:

1. Take twenty minutes every evening to read an enjoyable book in bed before sleep. Perhaps light a candle, settle in comfortably, and deliberately give yourself permission to forget about everything else but your book.
2. Take five minutes or so after completing your day's work to lie flat on the floor, breathe deeply, relax, and do nothing. Imagine a warm, glowing light washing over you and removing all traces of stress and worry from the day just gone.
3. Go for a walk every evening after dinner with your dogs and make a point of noticing all the little signs of the season in nature around you, enjoying the sights, smells, and sounds, perhaps even taking a few moments to rest with bare feet on the grass before going home.
4. Make your morning shower your special sanctuary time, and mentally prepare for the day ahead by repeating positive affirmations to yourself.

Perhaps you could use high-quality soaps and shampoos that you love, and take your time to feel clean, refreshed, and pampered.
5. Wait till you've put the kids to bed, then put on some good music and do some deeply relaxing stretching in your living room.

You do not need to spend money or do anything unusual to build stress management into your daily routine. In fact, it's better to do little but do it often. Try to incorporate as many five-minute windows of relaxation all throughout your day as possible—and the easier they are, the better. That said, you can also derive benefit from less frequent and more intensive relaxation efforts, such as a weekly massage, taking short weekend trips away, or a meditation retreat.

The 4-7-8 Breathing Technique

The best stress management techniques are those that are easy, simple, and can be done anywhere for any length of time. Nothing could be easier and simpler than a breathing exercise, and Dr. Andrew Weil (2015) has a great stress-relieving breathing exercise he likes to teach his patients.

The technique is straightforward: You inhale for the count of four, hold your breath for the count of seven, and finally exhale slowly for the count of eight. This breathing pattern resembles certain pranayama techniques from yoga and can be incredibly relaxing. It might not seem like much, but this particular ratio of inbreath to outbreath can quickly activate your parasympathetic nervous system and counter the fight-or-flight mode of chronic stress. What's more, it can be used either in the "heat of the moment" during stressful situations, or more as a preventative measure and everyday mental health maintenance routine.

While there are variations on this style of breathing, don't worry about getting things exactly right—any focused, slowed breathing will help calm you down, and as mentioned before, rest is not something to try to optimize! That said, here are a few things to keep in mind:

- Make sure you're sitting or lying comfortably
- Exhale through the mouth and inhale through the nose
- As you exhale, you can try making an audible "whush" sound
- You can breathe this way for as long as you like, but try to do a minimum of four or five cycles

You may be surprised at just how much calmer you feel after just a few cycles of breathing this way. Try the technique whenever you notice yourself becoming irritable or overwhelmed, or use it to disrupt an anxiety spiral before it spins out of control. You can use this technique as a kind of "brake" that interrupts not just the physiological cascade of the stress reaction, but everything that stems from it, including your automatic negative thoughts, feelings and behaviors.

The technique is great for use when driving, just before a nerve-wracking speech or presentation, during exams, in the morning to prepare for the day ahead or in the evening to process what's already transpired, in the gym, or combined with any other mindfulness activity like walking or yoga.

Of course, good stress management includes taking active steps in life to reduce sources of stress, and learning to be resilient. But neither of these can be done unless you're feeling calm enough first. The above breathing exercise is always a great move no matter what you choose to do next.

The Social Brain is a Happy Brain

In the previous section, we explored the ways in which our body's useful stress response can sometimes work against us. Learning to understand why we stress and how to counter it is a big part of keeping the brain healthy. That's because the stress response is an intrinsic part of the brain's functioning and is there for a reason. When we learn to work *with* our fight-or-flight responses and consciously moderate the arousal of our HPA axis, we experience less stress and more resilience.

In the same way, the human brain was built to be social. The brain evolved mechanisms to keep it safe in a dangerous and unpredictable world, but it also evolved sophisticated mechanisms to help it find purpose, connection, and meaning in its *social* environment. It may seem too strange to think of this way, but your ability to communicate, to empathize, to form bonds, to resolve conflict, and to "find your tribe" may be as important for your survival and well-being as a well-functioning immune system or a nutritious diet.

In the same way as the brain's methods of self-protection can sometimes backfire, however, our interactions with our social world can themselves become a source of stress. While most of us can agree that time spent in good company is life-giving and stress relieving, we have to admit that difficult relationships, conflict, and disharmony can all be *sources* of stress.

There is growing research demonstrating that the social brain is a happy brain (Felix et al. 2020; Hackett et al. 2019) with one study showing that loneliness can increase the risk of dementia by up to 40 percent! Strong social connections can improve attention and memory, slow cognitive decline, and keep us sharp. Yet in the long wake of the Covid pandemic, many of us are feeling more isolated than ever before—and so-called "social" media may be adding to the damage rather than alleviating it.

Yet again we encounter the kind of vicious cycle that may keep us trapped in habits that harm our brain health. We may feel lonely and isolated, and in time this lack of connection can start to impede our functioning. This impeded functioning makes us even less likely to reach out to others, and less sure of our ability to communicate well, so we withdraw further and the isolation increases. It can be a surprise to find that your social skills can atrophy in the same way as any muscle can if not used for a time. It's a mistake, however, to let being a little out of practice discourage you from reaching out.

How to Reconnect

You could have the healthiest diet, the perfect exercise routine, and a solid sleep schedule, and yet undo all your hard work by depriving yourself of connections to others. If this is an issue for you, don't worry—loneliness and alienation are far, far more common than most of us like to admit. Drastic overnight changes are unlikely, so be patient with yourself and simply commit to making small, realistic changes to your life where appropriate. Here are a few ideas.

Check In on Old Friendships

You don't have to start from scratch. Instead, rekindle old connections, especially those that may have faded a little over time. People can be busy and distracted, but sometimes the smallest effort can be rewarded—a simple text message can get the ball rolling. Be patient and try not to get discouraged if you need to work hard to re-establish a stale connection—it will be worth it in the end.

Stay Open-minded

You may have very real and insurmountable obstacles to socializing in the way you want to or think you should—but you can also experiment with socializing in ways that you might not have considered before. Older people can find their social lives reinvigorated when they overcome their fear of online communication or social media, but by the same token, younger people can surprise themselves by trying out "old-fashioned" things like going to church, volunteering, or joining a book club.

Stay open-minded about the forms your social connections can take, rather than giving up if things are inconvenient. For example, friends may live too far away to visit regularly, but why not video call them? You may feel that you don't have enough money to join hobby groups or have expensive nights out, but that doesn't mean you can't get involved in free community projects and groups. People are everywhere, and opportunities to socialize are everywhere—you may just need to shift your expectations about what "being social" might look like.

Put Quality Over Quantity

While a social brain is a happy brain, there is also some truth in the adage that "hell is other people." A 2021 study published in the *Journal of the American Heart Association* (Wang et al.) found that women who reported high "social strain" actually demonstrated poorer cardiovascular health than those who didn't. In other words, a big social life isn't automatically a healthy one—quality matters.

The secret to a *satisfying and healthy* social life is to prioritize genuine interactions, rather than merely seeking to add more random people to your life. Each of us has their own loneliness threshold as well as their own personal limit for what they consider to be "over socializing." Find your optimal range and take the time to fill your world with people you sincerely connect with. They don't have to be identical to yourself, and you don't need to have a perfect relationship, but they should make your investment of time and energy worthwhile. One or two very close friends is preferable to a big crowd that only stresses you out!

Change Your Mindset

A 2018 survey (di Julio et al. 2018) revealed that around one fifth of adults in the US, UK, and Japan said they "often or always feel lonely, feel that they lack companionship, feel left out, or feel isolated from others." Another study focusing on Americans reported that 61 percent felt lonely sometimes or always (Cigna Loneliness Index 2020). While there are many theories about why people feel so lonely when the world is more connected than ever before, one likely factor is what many call a "me-first mentality."

Socializing, like any other skill or human activity, takes practice, patience, and effort. Yet many of us approach social interaction with high expectations for reward but low or non-existent willingness to contribute anything ourselves. We may unconsciously see others as resources, or our connection to them as measurable only in terms of our personal benefit. The consequence is that when interactions require a little compromise, compassion, flexibility, or patience, we bail and look for what we want elsewhere.

Though unflattering, if this rings a bell for you, try to remind yourself that socializing may take time, and you may need to learn to harmonize with others not in spite of their differences, but because of them. "Self-care" is wonderful, but experiment now and then with care for *others*—family, your community, even people who don't necessarily "deserve" it!

Develop a thick skin where "awkwardness" is concerned, and try to be tolerant of people, who are likely also struggling to connect in an increasingly complex and divided world. The trick may be not in finding your perfect friends, but rather in learning how to see the good in the people who are already under your nose.

Laugh It Off!

Have you ever wondered about the *biology* of laughter?

It's easy to imagine the physical effects of anxiety on the body, but *all* our emotional states manifest in our bodies, and laughter is no different. Laughing is a complex orchestra of brain and body responses. Whenever you find something funny, a particular emotional response is triggered in your limbic system, which is implicated in how you process sensations like pleasure and well-being. From there, your motor cortex is activated, and this triggers the involuntary contraction of deep muscles, so you find yourself giggling and chuckling.

Sophie Scott is a professor of cognitive neuroscience at University College London, and she says that laughter is characterized by quick contractions of the rib cage and involuntary expulsions of air. But you already knew that. This process, while pretty funny in itself, actually releases endorphins in the body, increases oxygen intake, and leaves you feeling happier and more relaxed.

Though it might not seem like it at first, laughing is one of the body's most sophisticated techniques for self-regulation, not to mention the role it plays in fostering social bonds, relieving tension, and boosting resilience in the face of life's challenges.

Loretta Breuning, author of *Habits of a Happy Brain*, agrees, and explains how laughing can act as a kind of prophylactic against anxiety. Laughter acts like a pressure-release valve that counterbalances the damaging effects of too much cortisol in the body. Laughing helps us to feel good enough to be able to face our problems, seek information, and find a way out of negativity—rather than be swallowed by it.

How many times have you managed to completely shift your own perspective on a problem by simply choosing to see the "funny side"? The power of laughter is the ability it gives you to quickly switch your perception, shake off anxiety, and look at things afresh. This is because the trigger for finding something amusing actually comes in the way your brain processes information, interprets it, and gives meaning to neutral stimuli. When you laugh at something hilarious, all parts of your brain are engaged, and your entire body, including your blood vessels, lungs, and muscles, are recruited. Laughing is a full-brain, full-body experience.

To make the best of this natural brain-balancing superpower, you can deliberately find ways to bring more humor and laughter into your own life.

Keep a Store of Comedy for When You Need It

You've probably heard the advice to stock your kitchen with healthy snacks so that when you're feeling munchy, you can quickly grab something that will satisfy the craving and give you the boost you need. Well, you can think of comedy in the same way—almost as a kind of "brain supplement" to use whenever you feel a little low or stressed out. Keep a collection of funny videos or images on hand that always make you smile. You could try making funny playlists on your phone or collect favorite movies or TV show episodes that always cheer you up. Alternatively, buy tickets for a comedy night anytime you're feeling a little stressed—as far as healthy living habits, this one is likely to be one of the most fun!

Keep It Good-natured

A lot of what passes for comedy in the world is actually closer to cynicism. You know the kind of thing: sneering, being a little judgy, or poking fun at others. Though we may categorize this kind of thing as humor, it's quite distinct from the purely involuntary physical state of laughter described above—and therefore lacks brain-boosting and health-giving qualities. Be careful of using fake laughter, sarcasm, bitter humor, or "dark" forms of humor such as self-deprecation that may well be witty but don't produce a genuine physiological response.

Don't Worry About What's Appropriate

What do you personally find amusing? Embrace it! There really is no point in stifling laughter or judging your own personal preferences when it comes to humor. You don't need to justify, explain, or apologize for what tickles your funny bone. It's hard to explain why something is funny—so don't bother. In fact, part of the power of humor is its ability to release tension around social expectations or gently poke at norms and conventions.

Don't be self-conscious and, at the same time, accept that other people may laugh at things you don't quite get, either. As Breuning says in her book, "laughter is the release of fear." It may literally be the clearance of cortisol and tension from the body. Feeling self-conscious and embarrassed will only undermine that release.

Laugh When Things Are Tough

Sure, we laugh when we're having a good time, but laughter also serves an important function as a modulator for stress—even extreme stress, if necessary. Don't hesitate to laugh in very difficult or challenging situations—that's where laughter can be its most effective.

For anthropologists, laughter is a human universal that provides definite survival advantages. Chief Medical Correspondent Dr. Sanjay Gupta told CNN that in ancient human history, "laughter was the glue that kept the group together. The idea was that laughter was an external signal that can tell the group everything is okay, we can relax. [There is] no need to be anxious or threatened by what's happening around us. And so this would really be a great survival tool for groups of humans."

Don't be worried about laughing in the midst of dark times or even during an emergency—this may be a great sign of mental resilience, not to mention a great way to defuse social tension and signal the possibility of coping. There's a reason that good humor is so often given as an attractive quality in a potential mate; it's because someone who can laugh at life and themselves is demonstrating a certain strength of character and an ability to not let life get the better of them.

Dancing Can Boost Serotonin Levels

We'll now consider one final unexpected source of brain health and resilience, and that's dancing. Naturally, all physical movement strengthens the body's muscles and bones, oxygenates the tissues, and boosts blood flow—but there is something particular about this kind of movement that has additional benefits for the brain.

A 2008 study in *Scientific American* argued that movement that is synchronized with music actually activates reward processes in the brain and triggers what they call "pleasure double play." While the music and rhythm stimulate the brain's reward system (there's dopamine again), the dance itself activates sensory and motor circuitry. The feeling of interconnectedness of body and mind can be a rewarding and satisfying sensation in its own right, and especially pleasurable when combined with social activity that strengthens bonds and relieves stress in a group setting.

While you are busting a move on the dance floor, your motor cortex is hard at work planning and executing your movements, and a complicated interplay of coordination and control is underway. Your basal ganglion helps you keep things smooth, and your cerebellum helps integrate it all, including your incoming sensory data that tells you when the music changes, or someone else makes eye contact and comes to join you.

Researchers at Minot State University found in 2012 that Zumba classes actually improve participants' cognitive skills and their mood, and that the act of keeping up with a Zumba class helped people cultivate better decision-making, long-term memory, executive function, and visual pattern recognition.

In just an hour of dancing, your entire body rises to the challenge: Your breathing rate increases, your blood flow is boosted, your tension releases, and your brain actually creates new neural pathways. Your body floods with serotonin and endorphins, and if you combine dancing with socializing and a good helping of laughter, you have a potent recipe for total brain well-being.

Many of us can appreciate the need to stay mentally limber, but we may forget that brain agility and flexibility also comes from physical mastery and integration. Dance can be a rigorous brain workout for so many reasons:

- By learning choreography, we strengthen brain-body awareness and

coordination. We also boost our memories.
- By breaking out of a rut and trying something new, we halt rumination and anxiety and counteract depression (Jingu and Sungwoon 2007).
- By working together with others, we build our social skills and sense of connection and belonging.
- By expressing ourselves, we build self-esteem and even overcome social anxiety (Salo 2019). Loosening up can build social confidence and help us overcome inhibition—some people find that dancing makes them better at public speaking!
- By learning to be better dancers, we build concentration, greater conceptual understanding of movement and expression, and a certain "embodied fluency" that means stronger and livelier brains.
- By challenging ourselves to coordinate and learn something new, we build neural connectivity and stabilize our neurotransmitter levels (Goodill 2016). This is why "dance therapy" exists as its own form of treatment for mental illness.
- In the long term, dance can foster discipline and a sense of achievement,

not to mention patience, discipline, and the ability to self-reflect.

A long-term dance habit has been shown specifically to increase cortical thickness, boost brain plasticity, and increase activity in areas responsible for auditory and motor functions. Dance may even counter the effects of neurodegeneration or injury (Nahum et al. 2013) and offset cognitive decline in elderly people (Ramanoël et al. 2018).

That dancing can improve physical health and bring enjoyment is not under question. But if you'd like to take up dancing in order to boost *brain* health, then here are some great ways to get started.

Go with Whatever You Like!

You need to enjoy the dance and the music that accompanies it. Choose a dance form that you sincerely enjoy, whether that's jazz, hip hop, ballet, salsa, ballroom, or just freestyling it in your living room.

Consider Connecting with Your Culture or Your Community

Traditionally, dancing plays an important and specific role in human life. Since time began, human beings have used dance to express themselves, to mark important occasions, to celebrate, to flirt, to honor their tradition and heritage, to bond with one another, to participate in the religious and transcendental realm, or even to intimidate enemies in war (as the indigenous Māori of Australia do!).

You may derive extra benefit from dance if you can connect more broadly with its *meaning*. Choose a dance form that you find especially aesthetically pleasing or one that relates to your own cultural heritage. You may feel even more well-being, connection, and inspiration if you choose dance that is culturally embedded this way. At the very least, joining a local dance community is not unlike initiation into a mini tribe!

Dance Wherever You Can

You don't need a formal occasion . . . you don't even necessarily need a dance partner, a teacher, or a class. If you want to play around with dance on your own terms, start out with YouTube videos to get a sense of what you enjoy (Zumba is a great idea *and* a good cardio workout), or consider trying live Zoom classes.

It's great to have a regular dance routine (say, an hour or two every week), but that doesn't mean you can't enjoy a spontaneous jam session in the kitchen while you wait for the microwave to ping, or a little shimmy on the stairs when your favorite song suddenly comes on the radio. If you're feeling down, put on some good music and let it go!

Start Small and Have Fun

If full-on dance is not completely accessible to you or you're a person who considers themselves to have two left feet, don't worry. Don't be hard on yourself, and remember that all dance—professional, recreational, or something in between—feels good to your body and brain and will help cultivate well-being.

If dance is not quite your thing (yet), then experiment with other brain–body connecting activities such as Tai Chi, yoga, or simple stretching in your own way to enjoyable music. If you're not ready to get out there and dance in front of others, just practice on your own doing as much as you can.

Summary:

- One of the biggest threats to our brain's health and resilience is chronic stress. Stress is the body's reaction to challenges and demands in the environment and is a part of life. We need to learn to manage and work with stress, however, to keep levels healthy. Stress is only a problem if the body is never allowed to return to baseline.

- Cultivate your own resilience and coping. Take realistic steps to reduce stress triggers, learn to recognize when you're overwhelmed so you can take time to unwind, and practice mental toughness to endure adversities and discomforts that you cannot change. Create your own stress management ritual that fits your life.
- Try the 4-7-8 breathing technique: Inhale for the count of four, hold your breath for the count of seven, and finally exhale slowly for the count of eight.
- The brain is built to socialize, so make sure you're connecting well with others. Check in with old friends, stay open-minded about the people in your world, and let go of any "me first" mindset. People are everywhere, and opportunities to socialize are everywhere, but you may need to shift your expectations. Be patient.
- Humor and laughter have profound effects on brain health, so make sure to build in plenty of fun as part of your brain health regime. Finally, dancing can also boost serotonin levels, amongst its many other body and brain health benefits. Experiment with whatever form works for you.

Chapter 3: The Storytelling Brain

Human beings—or more accurately human beings' *brains*—are storytelling machines. The way we interpret life, the assumptions and expectations we hold, the narratives we construct for ourselves, and the words we use to speak to ourselves prove that one of the brain's primary forms of expression is verbal.

Words matter because they reveal the hidden ways we make sense of the world around us. While we can use words to express our reality, the truth is that words can in turn *influence us* and shape that reality. The words we surround ourselves with, the quality of the stories we immerse ourselves in, and the way we speak (to ourselves especially!) has a major impact on how our brains work. This relationship is not a theoretical one but rather something that we can see reflected in the brain itself, its activity, and its neurotransmitter levels.

In this chapter, we're going to be exploring the two-way verbal relationship that exists between us and the world.

Journaling Rewires the Brain

There is something very special about sitting down and putting pen to paper. The act of cracking open a notebook and filling it with your thoughts has far-reaching benefits—and these are not merely anecdotal but increasingly supported by neuroscience research.

Why is journaling so good for your brain?

Journaling De-stresses You

When you put your thoughts and feelings into words, you externalize them (i.e., get them out of your head) and immediately gain some psychological distance. This alone makes them feel less intense, and at once you give yourself the opportunity to think about your feelings, rather than remaining lost and reactive *inside* your feelings (Wapner 2008).

The amygdala in the brain is responsible for the complicated processes associated with emotional regulation, but one thing is for sure:

Emotional reactions are often lightning fast and involuntary. Writing, however, gives us a moment to interrupt this knee-jerk response, slow down our thought processes, and think more clearly. This reduces our anxiety levels, increases our feelings of self-awareness, and builds mastery and self-efficacy as we realize that we are actually able to *choose* our reaction to life situations.

A study done by Michigan State University found that writing reduces "cognitive load" (Schroder, Moran, and Moser 2017). According to the study's authors, chronic worriers actually impair their own cognitive function because they're essentially multitasking all the time! Journaling allows you to free up cognitive resources that you would otherwise spend on rumination and vague worry, and channel it toward something useful—like working through problems or processing emotions.

The research team was interested in what they called "expressive writing"—which is delving into your deepest thoughts and feelings. There may be relief in "setting aside" worries in this way. It's a little like telling your brain, "You don't have to keep thinking about this anymore, brain. It's been noted. It's here on the page, so you can let it go. Thank you for your help."

There's also something to be said for the power of labeling: When you put a succinct label on an emotion, it suddenly becomes smaller, more definite, and more manageable. Labels allow you to talk about your experience, describe it to others, and, in way, feel validated that your feelings are not beyond human understanding but make enough sense that human language can capture it.

While a single journal entry can affect your neurotransmitter levels and overall stress markers, the greatest benefits come from a consistent journaling practice.

Journaling Improves Your Memory and Comprehension

Journaling can improve your overall cognitive functioning (Sleister 2014). A 2021 University of Tokyo study published in *Frontiers in Behavioral Neuroscience* concluded that writing on physical paper has benefits when compared to using tablets or word processors. The theory is that physically interacting by hand with paper and ink supplies the brain with complex tactile and spatial information—the friction of the pen nib on the paper, the weight of the pen, the muscle coordination required to form letters, and so on. All this additional stimulation leads to greater brain activity and better encoding of memories.

Professor Kuniyoshi L. Sakai explains that, "Actually, paper is more advanced and useful compared to electronic documents because paper contains more one-of-a-kind information for stronger memory recall." While this strongly suggests that written notes and study materials are superior for memorization and learning, there are also benefits for overall brain health and psychological well-being. Staying more physically connected to your written expression gives it a more vivid, concrete being that may translate to deeper engagement, more creative thinking, and more grounded problem-solving. If you've ever "journaled" using a tablet or a desktop word processor, you now know why it doesn't quite seem the same as doing it by hand!

Journaling Can Foster Gratitude Feelings and Altruism

Gratitude journaling has been popular for some time, and the reasons are obvious: By taking the time to pause and consider just how many good things there are in your life, you can gently shift your perspective, boost your mood, and lower stress levels. Again, dopamine and serotonin are powerful brain chemicals that create feelings of well-being and combat fatigue and anxiety. This is not all about the warm fuzzies, however—increased well-being also primes you to make better choices, overcome adversity, and build resilience in the face of loss or disappointment.

Like humor, gratitude is an optimal mind state that you can switch into at any time. Recall that the fight-or-flight response pushes the brain into panicky, *narrowed* attention and knee-jerk self-protection; gratitude can be a clever way to counter this narrowness of attention on threat and danger. By deliberately choosing to pay attention to what you can be thankful for, you actually become better able to spot solutions, opportunities, and instances where your pessimistic predictions are actually not accurate.

University of Oregon researchers found that gratitude journaling is so effective at reducing one's perceptions of lack and threat that it increases altruism (Karns et al. 2017). Participants were first assessed for their baseline altruism levels and then underwent MRI brain scans. Half the group practiced gratitude journaling, whereas the other half didn't. The gratitude group demonstrated more altruistic responses to prompts and questions about charitable situations—and even their brains showed a difference in ventromedial prefrontal cortex activity, proving that gratitude is not just a nice feeling, but something that directly influences the brain.

Journaling Changes the Way You Think

The brain is neuroplastic. By journaling, you are exploring and encouraging new neural pathways—and these pathways strengthen with emotion and the increased dispersal of serotonin and dopamine. If we consider that a journal is a little like an "external brain," then we can see journaling as a means of articulating what's in our minds, editing it, rewriting it, and experimenting with new possibilities.

Whether we primarily use journaling for expression, reflection, planning, problem-solving, or simply venting (or a mix of all of these!), it can be a way for us to be more deliberate and conscious about how we're thinking. This fosters greater self-awareness and self-knowledge and reminds us that just as we're in control of the "story" we tell on the page, we are also in control of the stories we tell in our heads and the words we use.

Thus, journaling can be a way to process trauma and strong emotion, or a way to calmly and clearly work through a difficult decision. It can be used to make a list of achievements, plans, and affirmations, or it can take the form of a mind map that helps you tease apart the various factors in a troubling situation.

One underappreciated advantage of journaling is that it also boosts your emotional literacy—i.e., you become better at expressing your own internal state. This means you become better at communicating that state to others, and this will immediately improve your relationships and social skills (Bailkie and Wilhem 2015; 2018).

How to Start Journaling

First things first, a journal is NOT something you create for anyone's eyes but your own, and that means it doesn't have to be neat, organized, or pretty. Don't worry too much about doing it "right" and instead just experiment with different techniques and approaches that appeal to you. Here are a few ideas to get you started.

Choose Paper if Possible

You can certainly journal with a word processer if you like, but give pen and paper a chance, too. This gives you plenty of freedom to quickly annotate notes, switch up colors, and add doodles and other creative elements to enhance your expression. You could commit to a good-quality, attractive journal, or (if you're like some people) find a cheap, disposable journal that you don't mind messing up!

Keep it Consistent

You don't have to sit down and write a novel in one sitting. It's more important that your journaling is a natural and easy part of your everyday routine. Add it to another habit you do daily, or try to incorporate it into a meditation practice, alongside an exercise routine, or as part of your morning/evening rituals. Just aim for ten minutes or so every day and go from there.

Try a Simple Daily Structure

If you're stuck with what to write, consider creating your own formula. Pick three or four of the following elements to include in every entry:

- Quickly scribble down everything that's bothering you and get it out there on the page ("expressive writing"). As you do this, imagine you're releasing tension and offloading. Put words to your emotions. See how the word on the page bothers you far less when it's "out there" rather than "in here."

- Write down three to five things you're grateful for, or which provided you with joy and appreciation in the last twenty-four hours (try not to list the same things over and over). You could also list achievements, people you love, and little moments of happiness you experienced recently.

- Take a moment to reflect on your overall intentions for the day. Anticipate challenges ahead and decide how you'll approach them. Make broad plans and possibly jot down some affirmations or reminders of your bigger motivation. What brain state do you want to maintain for the day ahead?

- Reflect on the day past and ask yourself what you'd like to do better tomorrow. Celebrate small wins and let go of little disappointments and failures. Let this reflection guide your goal setting going forward.

- Include poetry, inspiring quotes, sketches, or contemplations that help you understand and process your emotions.

It's a great idea to have a consistent routine and structure to the way you journal, especially because this will allow you to spot emerging patterns over time. The more data you gather over time, the more you improve your self-awareness. That said, you don't need to make journaling a boring chore. It's okay to not journal every day, and it's okay to switch things up according to what else is going on in your life. Just remember that you are writing for yourself and not for an audience (even a hypothetical audience you're carrying in your own mind!). Write freely and don't judge or evaluate what you write—*the point is the process, not the outcome.*

The Neuroscience of the Reading

The brain doesn't just benefit from writing down its own stories . . . it benefits from reading stories, too. Most of the time, interest in reading has come from an appreciation of how the *content* of what we read can enrich our lives—for example, we can gain access to new knowledge and expose ourselves to novel perspectives and ideas we might not have otherwise.

But from a neuroscience perspective, reading is valuable not only for its content but for the mental processes it encourages. Reading changes the way the brain actually works and has a host of benefits over and above the ones we're all most familiar with.

According to Jessica Stillman in Inc., reading is a little like an "empathy workout" in that it challenges you to inhabit different narrative perspectives. This ability to use imagination and story to access the worlds of others doesn't just make you more understanding of others—it can also give you the chance to "try out" that perspective for yourself, such as when you read a story written in first person ("I thought to myself...").

Reading strengthens your focused attention, encourages your memory and ability to visualize, and literally rewires and restructures the shape of your brain. Harvard professor and author Joseph Henrich explains the mark that reading leaves on your brain, saying,

> "This renovation has left you with a specialized area in your left ventral occipital temporal region, shifted facial recognition into your right hemisphere,

> reduced your inclination toward holistic visual processing, increased your verbal memory, and thickened your corpus callosum, which is the information highway that connects the left and right hemispheres of your brain."

Granted, your brain might have had to do a little work with that paragraph! But the gist is clear: When you read, your brain launches into a frenzy of activity as it translates the marks on the page into letters, words, sentences, and ultimately whole worlds of meaning. There are countless cognitive and linguistic processes involved—semantics, phonology, orthography—that draw on multiple highly evolved areas in the brain.

The visual cortex is recruited in recognizing the shapes and symbols, and areas in the parietal and temporal lobe are involved in converting that visual data into meaning. Language is one of our brain's most enduring achievements, and reading is a powerful way to flex that muscle.

By reading, you master your ability to retain complex details, conjure up vivid scenes in your mind's eye, anticipate cause and effect, look for patterns, and sustain concentration for long periods. Regular readers may find that the continued effort makes them more patient, more self-disciplined, and more open-minded. It's no wonder that great thinkers of all stripes have long pointed to reading as a lifelong habit that supports achievement and excellence in every area of life.

When you read a good book, the brain releases both dopamine and oxytocin, as your brain perceives a reward. Interestingly, the genre does matter. Literary fiction appears to be the best for improving the ability to understand and empathize with social situations, while non-fiction reading is associated with activity in the prefrontal cortex, which is an area of the brain connected to problem-solving and decision-making (Berns et al. 2013).

Whatever your chosen genre, however, reading is stimulating work for your brain and increases neuroplasticity and neural connectivity—i.e., the brain's ability to constantly reorganize itself according to the tasks to which it is most often exposed to. Reading may mitigate the development of dementia in older people by up to 47 percent (Su 2022)—meaning it really may be a question of "use it or lose it."

In a fascinating study involving fMRI brain scans and the behavior of the amygdala when reading "Descriptions of Supra-Natural Events" in Harry Potter books, the authors discovered the impressive power of fiction to recruit several areas of the brain. These included the inferior frontal gyri, bilateral inferior parietal lobules, the left fusiform gyrus, and the left part of the amygdala. Feelings of surprise and enchanted enjoyment, then, are actually visible in the brain as a complex symphony of heightened blood flow and activity (Hsu et al. 2015).

The state of enchantment and surprise conjured by novel imaginings is called "magical" by the study's authors, and this may not be an exaggeration. It's not hard to imagine how such feelings of awe, curiosity, and delighted interest could support learning, creative problem-solving, and resilience. We can almost imagine that the brain state induced by such reading is an antidote to the anxious, hypervigilant brain state most associated with worry and negativity.

Neurobiologist Natalie Philips led a research team to conduct a similar experiment—one of just many that represents an emerging field called "literary neuroscience." They found that while study participants were reading Jane Austen's *Mansfield Park*, fMRI scans revealed increased blood flow across the brain.

There was more, however: The subjects were first asked to read in a very leisurely way and then asked to switch to a more "critical" and focused reading mode. This latter mode resulted in even more blood flow beyond the areas associated with pure problem-solving. When people say that reading is "broadening" your horizons, they may be more accurate than they know, since deep, engaged reading can literally expand the range of activation in your brain.

"Everyone told me to expect these really, really minute and subtle effects," Phillips told NPR, "because everyone was going to be doing the same thing, right? Reading Jane Austen. And they were just going to be doing it in two different ways. [. . .] What's been taking us by surprise in our early data analysis is how much the whole brain—global activations across a number of different regions—seems to be transforming and shifting between the pleasure and the close reading."

Other researchers like Phillips are investigating the brain's response to complex literary inputs such as rhyme, meter, metaphor, and more, as well as comparing the relative differences between, say, Dr. Seuss and Dostoevsky. All of this is to say that while your choice of reading material matters, it also makes a difference *how* you read. Distracted, superficial skimming may naturally require far less from your brain. But new neurological doorways can open and magic can happen when you challenge yourself to dive more deeply.

"But I Don't Have Time to Read!"

There's no doubt that the modern world is filled to the brim with attention traps and invitations to distraction. Social media and increasingly truncated and dumbed-down internet content can fracture our attention levels and lead to shallow, one-dimensional reading. Though it may feel harder than ever to cultivate a proper reading habit, the fact is that reading can help fortify you against the onslaughts of information overload. Reading can build your patience and focus and help you tune out noise and interference—whether that's coming from the outside world or from inside your own head!

If you're out of the habit of reading, or never really took it up in the first place, rest assured that only a small amount of effort will pay big dividends. Simply start small and try to maintain your gains so that over time you are building a habit for reading that is so entrenched it feels more wrong *not* to read. Here are some helpful ideas to get you started.

Take Baby Steps

Begin with just five or ten minutes at first, then gradually work up to longer and longer reading sessions. Depending on the kind of book and your energy levels, you may even train yourself to read for uninterrupted periods of an hour or more—but don't beat yourself up if it takes time to get there.

If you're the kind of person with "reading commitment phobia" and you find the prospect of a massive novel quite intimidating, then start off with something lighter and easier to dip into as and when you can. Novellas or collections of short stories are ideal for this, or investigate writer's magazines and publications that contain fun mixes of all different types of literature.

Make Reading the Easy Choice

As with any habit, you want to try to reduce the degree to which you're relying on willpower alone. Try to set yourself up for success by actively removing distractions and temptations, like phone notifications. Place books in locations where you habitually tend to scroll through your phone or zone out in front of a screen. Every time you're tempted to mindlessly consume content that way, you'll have a book at the ready instead. You may find in time that the book doesn't seem like second prize at all! If you're quite a serious phone junkie, however, you might like to install a reading app and challenge yourself to read a few minutes of a book *first* before allowing yourself to do whatever else it is you were tempted to do.

You Don't Have to Spend a Lot

Reading must have one of the highest returns on investment of any self-improvement habit—especially because it can often be absolutely free. Don't feel that you have to splurge on many expensive new releases from bookstores. Instead, explore library options in your area, join a book-sharing scheme (or even agree to swap titles with a friend or two), buy cheap second-hand books (luckily, the classics are often the cheapest of all), or even consider sourcing online pdf versions of books that are in the public domain.

Commit to Making Time

It's probably true that right now, there aren't too many completely free spots on your day-to-day schedule that are begging to be filled with reading. It can seem difficult to find time. It's also true, however, that the time we do have is often being spent on activities we don't value that much. Challenge yourself to monitor how you spend each and every hour of every day for a full week. At the end of the week, tally up how much time you spent watching TV, scrolling, or just generally wasting time. You may be surprised by how high that number is!

Once you've identified time-consuming but unproductive daily habits, you can slowly start to repurpose that time to a higher end. Carry a hard copy of a book around with you wherever you go so if you have a moment in a waiting room or at a bus stop, for example, you can squeeze in a few minutes of reading. Slash your evening TV time by half and dedicate the other half to reading. If you have a habit of scrolling through your phone first thing in the morning, place a book on your bedside table and commit to reading that instead—you'll probably feel a lot better for the change.

Watch Your Language!

The old saying goes "sticks and stones may break my bones, but words will never hurt me." There is at least one neuroscience research study, however, that suggests that this isn't actually true. Words—both positive and negative words—can profoundly influence us both psychologically and physically.

In an intriguing paper titled "Do Words Hurt?" a team of researchers concluded that negative words can raise implicit processing (IMP) in the subgenual anterior cingulate cortex (sACC) in the brain, which subsequently triggers the creation of stress-inducing hormones (Richter et al. 2010). In a similar study, researchers found that negative self-talk was closely associated with the creation of anxiety in children (Lodge et al. 2018).

Our brains have evolved to be the highly sophisticated and complex organs they are today over millions of years. The older, more primitive parts still remain with us—the amygdala is one—and these parts could be said to act unconsciously. These ancient parts of the brain evolved primarily to promote survival, and their mechanisms are blunt but swift and highly effective at detecting threats. The trouble is, the threats they evolved to detect are no longer with us in quite the same way as they were thousands of years ago. The brain can sometimes have difficulty discerning the difference between genuine threats to survival and mere annoyances—like a late bus, an annoying colleague, or an inflammatory YouTube video.

What Lodge et al. discovered was that the old mechanisms for threat detection in the brain are so subtle and finely tuned that they may even register certain *words* as threatening enough to warrant the release of fight-or-flight hormones. By observing study participants' brains in fMRI machines as they responded to different words and phrases, they were able to notice chemical reactions that actually interfered with normal brain functioning. It's as though the machinery that helped our ancestors respond intelligently to dangerous wolves could also be triggered by the mere *word* wolf.

Naturally, our species would be in big trouble if we risked serious illness merely by acknowledging the existence of negative ideas, but the implications of the study are astonishing. *Prolonged* focus on negative words can over time damage the brain's structure and function just as surely as any other brain-damaging habit, like binge drinking or boxing.

One of the reasons that reading can affect the brain so powerfully is that as we read or write, we silently internalize the words and almost "speak" them to ourselves in our own inner voices. Of course, whenever we engage with our own stream of self-talk, we are doing precisely the same thing—except we are the authors of the language we hear.

Cognitive behavior therapy (CBT) makes the observation that our thoughts are a constant stream of words that we speak to ourselves. This stream of words is like an interpretive narrative voice that acts as an intermediary between the actual facts of life and our feelings about them. Rather than reacting to the stimuli of life itself, we really react to our own story about what those stimuli are and what they mean. It matters, then, if we are consistently using words that cast reality in a negative light.

Words *can* hurt you—over time the negative story that you tell on repeat can cement itself in your brain and become the very world you inhabit.

But if negative words can hurt, the good news is that positive words can heal.

Authors Dr. Andrew Newberg and Mark Robert Waldman explained in their book *Words Can Change Your Brain* that

> "by holding a positive and optimistic [word] in your mind, you stimulate frontal lobe activity. This area includes specific language centers that connect directly to the motor cortex responsible for moving you into action. And as our research has shown, the longer you concentrate on positive words, the

more you begin to affect other areas of the brain."

Elsewhere, they explain that "*a single word* has the power to influence the expression of genes that regulate physical and emotional stress."

The effect reinforces itself. The words you use change your brain, and when your brain changes, so does your perception and the way you interpret the world. This in turn alters the words you choose to describe and explain your experience, and over time, you reinforce longer-term physiological and even genetic changes. Thoughts and feelings become words, words become actions . . . and those actions influence our thoughts and feelings. Words, then, create your reality, and not in some abstract way, but *directly* via your physiology.

People are often advised to label things "challenges" rather than "problems" because of the change in perspective that this word choice creates. But your language choices can be more subtle and pervasive than this. Consider the following examples:

- During a difficult negotiation with a work colleague, you repeatedly use the word "we" and "us." Your colleague may not be aware that it's happening, but these words and their implications help

their brain release small amounts of trust-inspiring oxytocin. Instead of triggering threat states in them, you create a subtle brain environment that encourages safety and harmony. This tiny and almost invisible word choice can ultimately make an enormous difference in whether your colleague is able to "hear" you or not!
- If you constantly pepper your speech with strongly negative words—even in a joking way—you may unconsciously trigger associations and neurochemical reactions in yourself and others without realizing it. Repeatedly using words like "kill," "destroy," "crazy," or "hate" may stimulate the brain in undesirable ways, even if you're not being 100 percent serious. You might not *literally* mean it when you say, "God, I could murder you right now," but the words may still have a subtle effect on a visceral unconscious.
- The labels and names you give to a thing change how you understand that thing, narrowing your perspective so that eventually all you can see is the associations that go with that label. For example, if in your silent self-talk you frequently label yourself as "scared," then in time you might come to really

believe that you are. But what about if you took a different line and called yourself cautious, careful, or even prudent? Might you start to feel differently?

- It's not only the literal words you use but the way you put them together—as well as what you don't say. For example, when giving feedback, you could choose either to apologize heavily for pointing out flaws, or you could calmly and confidently list everything you liked, while staying silent about everything else. Two entirely different conversations may result.
- Consider the enormous difference between saying "I have to do this" and "I *get* to do this." Though there is only one word that is different, there is an entire world of meaning and interpretation behind that word. "Have to" creates a vision of a world of force, obligation, and drudgery. "Get to" implies a world of opportunity and possibility—even privilege.
- Even though you might put a big fat NOT before a word, your brain is actually not good at processing negative information this way—i.e., if you see the phrase "not ugly," you will not perceive this in a positive way but

will rather focus on the negative associations of the word "ugly." Simply say "pretty" and "not ugly" in your mind to yourself and you can probably *feel* that they are not the same.

- During a difficult conversation with someone you love, you might consciously choose to say something like, "I feel confused and upset right now, and I worry that you don't care about me anymore," instead of, "You're making me so upset right now. Why don't you care about me anymore?" The words are not all that different, but the latter phrase places blame, disrupts connection, and creates more anxiety. The former phrase, just in the way it's structured, actually produces less stress for you both and for the relationship. Language can create discord, increase tension, and elevate conflict—or it can create the possibility of genuine understanding.

Our words will always reflect our own unspoken biases and worldviews, but the relationship goes the other way too: By changing our words, we can subtly shift those biases and take on new worldviews. If you are dieting, you may stop yourself from saying, "I'm not allowed junk food," and instead see what it feels like to say, "I only like things that are good for me." Compare the power of "childless" and "childfree," or "cheap" versus "affordable."

Of course, there are some natural limits to the power of language to shape your reality. Calling a brain tumor "my new friend" may make you *feel* better, but it won't change certain facts! Nevertheless, we do possess extraordinary power in how we speak about something, interpret it, express it, and shape it narratively. Words are never neutral.

In addition to starting a journaling habit and being discerning about the kind of reading you take in, spare a thought for all the thousands of word choices you make throughout the day, every day. Imagine that the words in your environment constitute the programming language that your brain runs on. Words are not just words but instructions to your brain, which will dutifully respond by releasing the corresponding neurotransmitters and hormones.

It can take a long time to break a lifetime of bad language habits, so just start small and with a little curiosity about the way you use language right now. Notice not only your word choice and sentence construction, but also your tone and nonverbal expression. Commit to making small changes whenever you become aware of language that is less-than-helpful, whether you're speaking it out loud or simply saying it to yourself mentally. Make small tweaks and observe—how does it feel to use language more positively?

Summary:

- The words we surround ourselves with, the quality of the stories we tell, and the way we speak (to ourselves especially!) has a major impact on how our physical brains work.
- Journaling can help lower stress levels by creating psychological distance and reducing the intensity of emotions. It also helps improve memory, cultivates gratitude, allows for planning and organization, and helps challenge unhelpful ways of thinking. Keep a consistent journaling habit that works for you, and remember that the point is the process, not the outcome.
- Reading is a valuable life hobby not only for the access it gives you to new knowledge, but for the mental processes it encourages, and the resulting brain help it helps cultivate.
- Reading strengthens attention, memory, imagination, and empathy, and restructures the shape of your

brain. Reading boosts neuroplasticity and connectivity and makes people more patient, self-disciplined, and open-minded. A reading habit takes time to build; make small changes and stick to them until they become habitual.

- Words—both positive and negative—can profoundly influence brain health and consequently our psychological well-being. Negative self-talk can create real stress in the brain and undermine its function—but positive words can promote health and well-being. Pay attention to your language choice and how it affects your reality, your perception, and your emotions, then make conscious changes according to the kind of world you want to create for yourself.

Chapter 4: The Connected Brain

In this chapter, we'll take a look at the neuroscientific evidence for an idea that many of us have long suspected to be true: that kindness, generosity, and a life lived with purpose can have immense effects on your physical well-being. Self-help literature on boosting brain health often focuses on very limited ideals of what a healthy brain should be and do: It's all about intelligence, processing power, or problem-solving capacity.

And yet, if you were to ask a strong and healthy elderly person how they keep vital and mentally switched on, they probably won't tell you that the secret is sudoku puzzles and "brain workouts." Rather, they might mention their grandchildren, their volunteer work, or the strong sense of belonging they feel in their community. One of the biggest determinants not only of life satisfaction but longevity, too, is a life that feels like it means something. Let's take a closer look.

Your Brain Wants a Purpose

What makes a good heart?

That's easy: A healthy, happy heart is one that pumps well enough to supply fresh oxygenated blood to every tissue and organ of the body and also carries carbon dioxide back to the lungs so it can be removed. In other words, a healthy heart is one that does the *job* a heart should do.

In the same way, a healthy gut does what a gut should do, and healthy arms and legs do what arms and legs should do. When it comes to the brain, we can see its health in terms of its function. But then . . . what is the brain's function?

The brain is not like a heart or a stomach or a leg or an arm. It has many functions that are easy to identify—it can learn, solve problems, imagine, memorize, plan, etc. But to what end are all of those functions applied?

It seems as though the brain is an organ that doesn't just have a job, but a *purpose*. Those many functions need to be put toward some higher ambition. After all, a person may possess a vital, intelligent brain capable of many impressive functions, but if that brain continually asks itself, "What's the point?" it's hard to imagine that we would call it healthy.

A fascinating meta-analysis by *Ageing Research Reviews* strongly suggests that having a purpose in life is not just some nice lofty ideal, but absolutely necessary for good brain health (Bell et al. 2022). Without it, adults risk higher rates of dementia, not to mention depression. Researchers even hinted that purpose and meaning may be detectable in the body as a counterbalance to distinctive neuroinflammatory cellular stress response. The purposeful brain appears to be better connected and organized.

A research team at University College London crunched data from more than sixty-two thousand older people across three countries and found a negative correlation between what they call "positive psychological constructs" (PPCs) and cognitive impairment in later life. In particular, measures for "purposeful living" were better predictors of good cognitive health than other PPCs like optimism and happiness. This is an astonishing finding—*having a life of purpose may ultimately be healthier than having a life that is merely happy.*

One interesting study found that having a life of purpose didn't actually prevent Alzheimer's disease—rather it allowed people to function well cognitively despite autopsies after their deaths showing evidence of neurodegeneration (Boyle et al. 2022). This almost seems to be hard evidence for the famous Nietzsche quote: "He who has a why to live can bear almost any how." It is as though having a purpose mobilizes the brain toward that purpose, regardless of obstacles or adversity.

Georgia Bell, the team lead, explained that

> "people with higher eudemonic well-being may be more likely to engage in other protective behaviors, such as exercise and social interactions. Whilst an individual may gain happiness from these, the goal-oriented pursuit to live in a way that is purposeful [or] meaningful may act as motivation to live a healthier lifestyle."

Eudemonic pleasure denotes the satisfaction that comes with purpose and meaning, whilst hedonic pleasure comes from simply enjoying yourself. While hedonistic pleasures can certainly be fun, their benefits tend to be fleeting—and sometimes downright unhealthy. Eudemonic pleasures, on the other hand, meet deeper needs and may strengthen human beings in a more lasting way.

Again, purpose seems to come down to function. Human beings who are comfortable and have plenty of leisure may tick all the recommended lifestyle boxes, yet still have poor brain health and low levels of well-being, precisely because their lives are not *for* anything.

Here, we arrive at an interesting conclusion: Even our worldviews and life philosophies can have concrete physiological effects on the health of our brain. In other words, the tissues and neurotransmitters of the organ inside your skull can be protected and supported by such abstract things as having a sense of meaning, value, and direction in your life. A nutritious breakfast and regular exercise help, of course, and will assist with resilience, mental acuity, and overall cognitive health. But it's worth remembering what higher purpose all this well-being might be channeled toward.

Honoring Your Brain's Higher Reason

It's far easier to decide what to have for breakfast or how to exercise than to figure out your "life's purpose." And yet, there is some promising research that suggests that the things that leave people feeling most fulfilled are relatively predictable.

Focus on Relationships

The Harvard Study of Adult Development (see adultdevelopmentstudy.org) followed its participants for a whopping eighty years and came to a conclusion that will not surprise anyone: Longevity has a strong link to meaningful relationships with others.

Close family and friends, a sense of community, and knowing that you belong to a stable social group is a powerful protective against neurodegeneration. On the other hand, shame, isolation, and social disconnection can be as serious a risk factor for cognitive decline as smoking or obesity.

Think About Values, Not Goals

While people often get carried away thinking about New Year's resolutions, SMART goals, and setting intentions, it may actually be better for your brain to look at things in terms of purpose and meaning. While achieving a goal is no doubt satisfying, it's worth considering how smaller goals fit into the bigger picture of your life. Imagine that each smaller goal is like a bead—but your overarching purpose and meaning is the thread that collects all of those beads together into one necklace.

Your values are things that you never, ever compromise on. They can help you find clarity and direction, and this in turn can help you eliminate unnecessary stress and cultivate more trust in yourself. Your values could be things like, for example, independence, compassion, wisdom, honesty, resilience, service, adventure, or physical prowess.

Decide What You're Living For

Sounds pretty intense, but working this out for yourself just might be one of the best things you can do for your health—physical and mental. This is not about getting lost in deep philosophical questions; in fact, identifying your purpose is most often a question of real pragmatism.

It may be that you're devoted to your children and are committed to raising them as best you can. Or perhaps your purpose is a spiritual or religious one, and you want to find closer connection to the divine. Your purpose could be to help others, to explore and learn all you can about the world, to build useful things, or to create beauty wherever you go. Finally, realize that your purpose can and will change across the various stages of your life.

What If I Can't Find My Purpose?

Don't worry, you're not alone! It may be for a time that you need to have the purpose "find my purpose." Merely choosing to make this decision reorients you toward meaning, whether you "find" it or not. It sends a strong message both to others and to yourself that you intend to live life intentionally and with deliberation. Even if you're not 100 percent sure what that looks like yet, you will still feel more driven and focused because you will know that you're not living by accident, nor just existing from one experience to the next.

If you're still having trouble identifying something you're happy to call a purpose, that's okay—it may take time. Try to answer the following questions and prompts to see what insight they yield.

- Think of the last time you felt totally engaged, excited, and hyperfocused on a task. What was the task, and what made you so absorbed with achieving it?
- Thinking back on your life, what is one thing that you would never, ever do or think *no matter what*? Try to reflect on what this says about your deeper values.

- Who do you really admire and see as a hugely accomplished human being? Try to think of the qualities, actions, and worldviews these people demonstrate, and ask yourself if any of them apply to you, too.
- What do you consider the worst possible thing a person can be? Contemplate those things that truly disgust you and be curious about their opposites. For example, if you think that lying and deception are the worst, it might suggest that a purpose and value for you is honesty and truth-telling.
- Imagine that you have died, and you come back as a ghost to read your own obituary. What would have to be said about you for you to think, "Wow, I lived my life right"?
- Think back to when you were a very young child and try to remember the activities you were most drawn to and the role you most readily took on for yourself. Does this tell you anything about your deeper purpose?

Generosity Triggers the Happiness Trifecta

Human beings are social animals, and there's good reason to believe that our instinctive urge to help those who need it is not only about maintaining group cohesion, but an important part of *our own* well-being, too. There are some people who describe generosity in almost addictive terms, as though the high they get from making someone else happy is greater and more rewarding even than their own happiness. The euphoria from altruism may be more than just a turn of phrase and could be neurochemical—we can consider dopamine, serotonin, and oxytocin a kind of "happiness trifecta" created by kind and selfless acts.

From an evolutionary perspective, helping those around us can provide a powerful sense of purpose, joy, and well-being, plus a greater feeling of security in the world. Empathy, trust, and compassion offer real survival benefits. After all, groups of people who know how to resolve conflict, look out for one another, and work together are inevitably the groups that survive and thrive. All this is to say that there's a very good reason your brain rewards *you* with feel-good brain chemicals when you make someone *else* happy!

One of the ironies of the modern world's obsession with psychology and self-help is that it tends to turn attention inward and onto the self. While self-awareness is a valuable thing, the truth is that self-absorbed contemplation is often the last thing that makes us happy. Instead, many people are thrilled to discover that they feel best when they're not thinking about themselves at all.

If most of us are honest, however, generosity doesn't come naturally, and it may not be something we feel inclined to do. If we consider it, it's often for selfish reasons, i.e., we think, "Oh, great, being nice could reduce my chances of Alzheimer's disease. I guess it's time to volunteer at the old folk's home!" The power of generosity, however, is that it works best when attempted for genuine reasons— i.e., for the transcendent and redemptive power of sincerely making someone else's life better.

Make Giving an Everyday Habit

You don't need to become a full-time philanthropist and give away everything you own to start becoming a more generous person. In fact, smaller, more regular acts of kindness may paradoxically make a bigger difference. The form your kindness takes will likely depend on the need that you find around yourself. So, the first step to becoming more generous is to become more perceptive and aware of others and their experiences, then responding according to *their* need, rather than your perception of what you'd like to do for them. This makes you a more spontaneous and responsive giver.

So, for example, you may start paying attention to colleagues at work and notice that one of them has been especially overwhelmed and stressed. Without making a big display of it, you could step in and do one or two of their smaller tasks for them, just because. Or notice when someone's hands are full and hold the door open for them, or recognize that they seem a little down, so you compliment them on something they've done well. All of these things may take you just a few minutes at most but can make you (and them) feel like a million dollars.

The trick is not to have too limited an idea of what "generosity" means. Think about all the people in your life and what they may be going through right this moment. How could you help them? Think about the gifts you have, the things you know, and the skills you could offer, and become curious about who might need that right now. Even smiling at people and making friendly eye contact can be a powerful act of generosity. Recognize when people have made efforts and praise and compliment them. Show your gratitude (as you can imagine, gratitude and giving overlap significantly).

Even asking for help or advice can be felt as generosity. Get in touch with the older people in your life and ask them something only they would know, and then lavish them with plenty of appreciation and respect as they tell you. Giving and receiving, then, are sometimes divided by a very thin line, and you can compliment someone enormously by allowing them to shine in their own generosity.

More formal giving counts, too. Giving money is great, but giving of yourself, especially your time and kindness, is usually far more impactful for everyone involved. Share what you have—and that's not just material.

Michael Norton is a professor of business administration at Harvard Business School, and in 2008, he and his colleagues conducted a little experiment. They gave either five dollars or twenty dollars to study participants and told them to spend the money either on themselves or on someone else. They then checked in afterward to measure how each participant felt.

The people who spent money on others reported feeling better than those who spent it on themselves. Not only did the people who spent money on themselves feel less good overall, but spending twenty dollars on themselves did not make them feel any better than spending five dollars. This result held even though, when the researchers asked people to predict the results, they guessed that receiving would make them happier than giving (Dunn et al.).

Though neuroscientists aren't 100 percent sure what goes on in the brain when people act generously, the results of such studies do speak for themselves. Some studies have shown that older people who volunteer are 44 percent less likely to die in the following five-year period (Oman et al. 1999). Other research found a correlation between volunteering and happiness—and it's not because happier people tend to volunteer. In fact, the paper's authors calculated an "equivalent well-being value of 911 pounds (approximately 1,150 dollars) per volunteer per year on average to compensate for the well-being increase associated with volunteering." Another study coined the term "helper's high" (Dossey 2018), while a 2006 study using fMRI scans of brains showed definite activity in the decision-making prefrontal cortex and several other regions of the brain associated with reward and social attachment (Moll et al. 2006).

To conclude, people like giving. Their brains are built for it . . . and it's good for them!

The only thing standing in the way of us being more generous, kind, and altruistic people is, essentially, habit. Perhaps we have been indoctrinated to believe that the real goal of life is the pursuit of happiness . . . our happiness only. Or maybe we falsely believe that the world is a competitive, hostile place and the only way to survive is to constantly look out for ourselves and, well, be a little selfish.

But here we get a peek into why generous people may be happier and healthier—they do not live in these fear-directed and stressful states of mind, or at least they are not driven primarily by a "me first" attitude. When you think about it, being generous communicates to yourself and others a strong message of belief in your own well-being. It's as though you are saying, "I know I have enough. I'm okay. I can afford to give." This attitude is the flipside of the grateful attitude and explains how the more we give, the richer we feel.

If you can maintain a brain state that genuinely has you believing in your own good fortune, and you are not narrowly focused on competition, survival, or defense, then it's easy to imagine that you would feel calmer, more confident, and more content in life. The curious thing is that it's actually this state of mind that most primes you for success and achievement. Here are a few ideas for bringing a little more kindness to your life.

- Don't make charity automatic—a regular direct debit that you forget about is not likely to be all that impactful for you (although the donation will be appreciated).
- Choose causes that you are passionate about and align well with your values and your overall purpose. If you do this, it won't even feel like giving—it will feel like they are helping *you*!
- If you're feeling low and uneasy about something, ask what's missing . . . and then commit to giving that to someone else. If you're feeling unloved, show love to someone else. If you're feeling lost and confused, help someone find their way. If you're feeling afraid, comfort someone. If you're feeling depressed, do something to cheer

someone else up. It may sound strange, but it works like magic.
- Alternatively, if your negative inner voice is getting the better of you, just disengage with it entirely and focus yourself on other people and what's going on in their worlds. Sometimes, the best thing for rumination and self-absorption is distraction and reminding yourself that you are not the only person in the universe.
- When someone thanks you for your kindness, accept it simply and warmly, then move on. You don't need to downplay it or, on the other hand, pat yourself on the back for being awesome. Sincerely show your appreciation for their appreciation.
- Finally, give in a way that is meaningful to the receiver. What do they most want and need? And, importantly, in what form are they most able to receive it? For example, a close friend may become embarrassed if you openly offer them money to help with their financial troubles. Anticipate this and simply give them a completely anonymous donation. It will be the most thrilling secret you'll ever keep.

Self-compassion Is Important, Too

Your brain needs a purpose, and one of the most satisfying purposes it can have is to be useful, kind, and compassionate to others. In the final part of this chapter, we'll see that *self*-compassion is just as important for your brain health.

While most of us can believe that self-compassion makes us feel better, there is growing research to suggest that being kind to yourself has measurable effects on your health and physiological well-being—brain included. Self-compassion isn't just about the warm fuzzy feeling that comes with being nice to yourself; it also correlates with greater mental toughness, more motivation, less anxiety and depression, and more satisfying relationships.

Bearing in mind the almost toxic effects of stress hormones, and the danger of prolonged periods in fight-or-flight mode, it's no surprise that knowing how to soothe, forgive, and accept yourself can help you thrive and shake off the wear and tear of life's challenges.

The trick is that self-compassion is not a reward we grant ourselves for being "good enough" to deserve it. Self-compassion isn't conditional, and it's not something we indulge in when things feel like they're going well. Rather, self-compassion is an attitude we take to ourselves regardless of the difficulty we're having, independent of our flaws and weaknesses, and no matter how we may be feeling.

Self-compassion overlaps with acceptance: When we can embrace who we are and what we are really going through in life, we actually shift our perspective so that we can start thriving *despite* imperfections and difficulties.

If you're not in the habit of self-compassion, the whole concept can seem a little vague. Imagine it this way: Self-compassion is treating yourself as you would a loved and cherished friend experiencing the same thing you're experiencing. The way you'd talk to them is about recognizing their humanity, and the fact that even though people are flawed and make mistakes and suffer sometimes, that doesn't mean they are worth any less as human beings. Self-compassion is simply taking the same attitude to yourself.

Crucially, being kind to ourselves is not about being "positive" or pretending that things are better than they are. It's about taking a gentler attitude we take to reality and not trying to deny or interpret that reality in any particular way. For example, it may be true that your weight is starting to impact your health and that you need to make serious changes to your lifestyle and diet. There is a big difference, however, between saying, "You're a fat pig and you need to sort yourself out or you're going to die, and it'll all be your fault," and, "It's okay, we all have our struggles, and this is yours. Whatever happens, you have plenty of great qualities, and you matter."

In other words, you don't have to deny reality, lurch into self-pity, or engage in "toxic positivity" to show a little compassion for yourself. People may worry that being kind to themselves will undermine any motivation to change and improve, but it's probably the opposite—only when you can truly accept yourself as you are, in the here and now, are you empowered to start making changes. You don't have to hate yourself to change!

What's more, there are some things in life that we simply cannot change; sometimes the only thing we can do when faced with certain pains, losses, or discomforts is to accept them and refuse to add to our own misery by being unkind to ourselves on top of it.

Shifting Out of Fear Mode

Negative self-talk can release a steady stream of stress-creating neurochemicals and hormones in your body. The longer you remain in survival mode, the worse it is for your body, mind, and soul. Having your entire organism primed to detect and respond to threats is a metabolically expensive state to be in, and it has harmful effects on the body, especially when prolonged.

The key here is that the worst sources of this kind of stress are often not coming from our environment at all—but from *us*. If we bathe our brains in constant critical and hateful self-talk, we are engaging in the equivalent of constantly drinking small amounts of poison or living for years breathing in heavily polluted air.

Compassion is an antidote to this vitality-destroying stress. When we are kind—to ourselves and others—we stem the tide of stress hormones in the body and trigger the release of healing, repairing, and balancing chemicals instead: oxytocin, serotonin, dopamine, and endorphins. Self-compassion neutralizes the threat response and helps us feel a little more safe and secure in the world.

Self-kindness encourages the body to release oxytocin, which bolsters feelings of optimism and contentment, increases your resilience and coping, and helps you more quickly recover from disappointments. In a study published in *BMC Women's Health*, a research team found that women who practiced more self-compassion demonstrated lower levels of stress and depression, and a greater ability to focus on their work (Pires et al. 2018). The researchers even found that there was increased activity in the precuneus, which is a part of the brain associated with "self-referential processing" (we'll come back to the importance of this in a moment).

The truth is that self-compassion doesn't make you vulnerable, weak, or self-indulgent, but rather allows you to tap into a real source of strength and health. Don't believe that self-criticism is necessary for motivation. Just ask yourself who would be better at problem-solving, creative thinking, and living up to high standards—the person who is frazzled, burned out, self-hating, and unable to focus on anything but the negative? Or the person who is relaxed, calm, confident, and secure in who they are?

At the Self-Acceptance Summit hosted by *Sounds True*, Dr. Kelly McGonigal explained how we can develop what she calls a "self-to-self relationship." She encourages people to view themselves and their suffering from a distance. The ability to take this step back almost brings you out of your "suffering self" and into your "compassionate self." From there, you may be able to access more acceptance and think more clearly through problems. This is exactly the switch to "self-referential processing" discussed by Pires and her colleagues.

Here are a few ways Dr. McGonigal suggests you can begin making this shift and gently encourage your brain out of fear and threat and into calm acceptance:

- Write a letter to yourself, but do it in the second person, which means using the "you" perspective. For example, "Hi, Adam. I can see you are having a hard time right now; you're scared, I get that. I hope you know that you have a lot of people rooting for you, though . . ."
- Visualize your future self when you are very old and on your death bed. This future self is kind and wise and, with the power of hindsight, is looking back to your younger self. What do they say to you? Imagine a dialogue between you. What advice would they give?
- Embrace your imperfections and let go of the idea that you will someday be the kind of person who will never feel scared, lonely, angry, confused, or ashamed. Be okay with being in process, being incomplete, and being flawed. Try to look at yourself *as you are right now* and find that you are . . . enough.

- When looking at your mistakes, try to reframe them as learning experiences and see what they might be able to teach you. When looking at your flaws, try to imagine that they are what make you unique—and that you also have strengths that are worth celebrating!
- Create some "empathy statements" that you might use when showing kindness to others. Then, you guessed it, try to say these same statements to yourself—in a mirror if possible. For example, an empathy statement could be, "You're doing your best, and that's great," or, "Remember that you are loved and that you belong."
- If you're feeling a particularly strong negative emotion, realize that you don't have to stop it—just don't identify with it so strongly. Instead of saying, "I'm stupid," you could say, "I'm feeling stupid," or, to put even more distance between that feeling and yourself, say, "I'm feeling a little unintelligent *right now*." Imagine setting the experience off to the side and realize that you are having a feeling; you are not the feeling.
- Gratitude can help here, too. When you notice that you're beating yourself up, pause and deliberately switch your

focus. Think of three things there and then that you can be thankful for.
- Get into the habit of asking yourself, "What do I need now?" Instead of focusing on what you lack, what you can't do, what you're struggling with, or what you can't accept, consider yourself with care and concern and ask how you can help—without judgment.

Life can certainly be hard sometimes, so why make it even more difficult for yourself? When you judge yourself for your pain, you just add more pain. If we feel bad about feeling bad, we trap ourselves in reinforcing spirals of negative feelings—and none of it is necessary for us to be the best people we can be.

Self-compassion, then, is about giving up the struggle against yourself. You can still be effective, decisive, and motivated, and you can still push and challenge yourself, but you no longer need to do these things in an attempt to *escape* a self you dislike. Rather, you can move *toward* something positive, and your actions can be aspirational.

Summary:

- Kindness, generosity, and a life lived with purpose can have immense effects on your physical well-being and brain

health, as can self-compassion and acceptance.
- Our worldviews and life philosophies can have concrete physiological effects on the health of our brain; make sure you have a genuine sense of meaning and purpose to apply yourself to. Think about values, belonging, and social connections.
- Generosity triggers the release of oxytocin, dopamine, and serotonin and is great for brain health. Helping others can provide a powerful sense of purpose, joy, and well-being, plus a greater feeling of security in the world.
- Broaden your understanding of what generosity looks like, and be responsive to the needs of people around you.
- Self-compassion is also essential for brain health and helps us overcome adversity, relieve stress, and learn from mistakes. Being kind to yourself has measurable effects on your brain health and shifts you out of "fear mode."
- Negative self-talk can release a steady stream of stress-creating neurochemicals and hormones in your body, whereas self-compassion correlates with greater mental toughness, more motivation, less

anxiety and depression, and more satisfying relationships.

Chapter 5: The Disciplined Brain

What do you think of when you see the word "discipline"? Do you imagine the kind of toughness and self-restraint required to stick to a gym routine or stop yourself from indulging in a bad habit? Do you think of Navy SEALs or drill sergeants?

In this chapter, we'll be looking at a slightly different perspective on discipline, namely that *it's possible to discipline yourself to be happy*.

Many of us assume that our mood is not really under our control. We imagine, perhaps even unconsciously, that how we feel is nothing more than a result of the influences our environment has on us—if things are going well, we'll be happy, and if things aren't, we'll be sad or anxious.

Learning to Be Optimistic

But optimism can be thought of as a good habit—and one as nurturing for your brain as any other healthy habit, like keeping a good sleep routine or eating your veggies. The first thing to understand about optimism is that it's something we have a degree of control over. This is important because optimism can literally alter your brain.

A study from the University of Illinois at Urbana-Champaign examined the MRIs of sixty-one healthy participants and discovered that people with bigger orbitofrontal cortices (OFCs) on average seemed to be more optimistic and less anxious (Dolcos et al. 2015). An earlier study also looked at OFC size, but particularly in adults who had experienced an earthquake and tsunami in Japan (Sekiguchi et al. 2011). Their data showed that people who had lost the greatest amount of OFC volume showed a greater likelihood of being diagnosed with PTSD later on. Follow-up studies by the same researchers found tiny changes in participants' white matter integrity—suggesting that stress and trauma can damage the brain's interconnectivity.

We already know that stress can wreak havoc on the brain, and these studies show that there is indeed a link between brain health and optimism. But is the reverse true—i.e., can optimism change your brain in positive ways? The Dolcos study cautiously concluded that it could and suggested that optimism may protect a person against anxiety by creating changes in the OFC. When it comes to the brain, there are often chicken-and-egg questions about cause and effect, but there is good reason to expect that training yourself to respond well to stressful events can mitigate their effects on your brain.

Don't worry if you're a bit of a Negative Nancy. Licensed psychotherapist and licensed clinical social worker (LCSW) Karol Ward explains that optimism is down to both nature and nurture, saying,

> "From my experience, optimism is both a personality trait and a product of our environment. From an early age, babies and children pick up the emotional vibes in their homes. If the atmosphere is relaxed and loving, children blossom even if they innately have a tendency toward anxiety. But if the home environment is tense and filled with dysfunction, optimism is one of the first things to go. It's hard to be emotionally open and hopeful when that is not being modeled for you by your caretakers."

An interesting twin study suggested that optimism is only 25 percent heritable (Plomin et al. 1992), with other factors, including socioeconomic status and environmental factors, that are indeed out of most people's control. But that still means that we have some scope to deliberately cultivate optimism no matter our environment or history.

While some people may be optimistic by nature or may have had luck and opportunity on their side, other people can learn to become optimistic—and the trick is to realize that this is indeed an option!

First things first, optimism is not just being happy. Neither is it about being blindly positive about everything no matter what. Kimberly Hershenson, a licensed master social worker (LMSW), explains the difference.

> "Positive thinking doesn't mean that you ignore life's stressors. You just approach hardship in a more productive way. Constructing an optimistic vision of life allows one to have a full interpersonal world in spite of unfortunate circumstances . . . [It] reduces feelings of sadness/depression and anxiety, increases your lifespan, fosters stronger relationships with others, and provides a coping skill

during times of hardship. Being optimistic allows you to handle stressful situations better, which reduces the harmful health effects of stress on your body."

Optimism, then, is a constructive, *active* state of mind—it assumes not that everything is just fine, but rather that with effort, things can always be improved. It is not about what is perceived, but about the nature of the perceiving. It's the state of mind that acknowledges a person's power to act, to choose, to solve problems, and to cope with life's challenges. Optimism is not easy or foolish—in fact, it takes deliberation and courage to choose to see things in the most favorable light possible, and to consciously perceive things in a way that will most allow you to cope.

Optimists can see the bad in life just as well as pessimists can, but they have a different set of beliefs and expectations about what that negativity means and how much they are able to act to change it. Pessimists often claim that they are "realists," but the reverse may be true—optimists are oriented in such a way as to engage with reality in the most beneficial way possible. Pessimists adopt a perspective that doesn't do this—sometimes even thinking and behaving in ways that genuinely bring about the negativity they believe they perceive.

A study in *The Journal of Personality and Social Psychology* suggested that positive brain states are most often correlated with left-side brain activity, and vice versa (Tomarkin et al. 1990). The relationship goes the other way—by deliberately changing your brain state, you can alter the pattern of activity in your brain, presumably with long-term consequences.

A paper titled *Alterations in Brain and Immune Function Produced by Mindfulness Meditation* (Davidson et al. 2003) found that people could consciously shift brain activity to the right using mindfulness meditation. After two months' training, participants reported feeling happier and less anxious.

So, training to think on the (b)right side is possible, and it only takes the willingness to try and a little patience. Just because you have been pessimistic in your life so far, it doesn't mean you can't change. In fact, acknowledging the truth of this may be your first act as a voluntarily optimistic person! Here are some tips if you're feeling a little rusty:

Tip 1: Change perspective

The "glass half empty versus glass half full" phenomenon emphasizes that in both cases, it's the same glass. To be optimistic is to find a way to look at your life exactly as it is right now, but through a different lens. This doesn't even need to be "positive" so to speak, but just ask yourself, "Is there another way of looking at this?"

It may also help to simply imagine what an optimistic person would see, and try to pretend you are them for a moment. Remember that optimism is not about the events or ideas in question, but about your orientation to them. Try changing up your language or interpretation of events. Sometimes, this may just mean feeling *neutral* about something instead of assuming it's negative without any evidence.

Tip 2: Turn off the news, get off social media

The media's only aim is to drive engagement and capture your attention. It does this by making you feel as bad as possible, and it deliberately pushes on those fear/rage/disgust buttons that keep you watching. Be very careful about the kind of material you allow into your world, and moderate its effects by not spending too long on any one platform, channel, or site.

It's no exaggeration to say that twenty-four-seven media coverage of the state of the world can actually trigger genuine mental health crises in people; just unplug and take a step back. Remind yourself that the views you are seeing are imbalanced, and temper any feelings of powerlessness or despair by committing to small, realistic actions in your own world here and now.

Tip 3: Be discerning about the people you surround yourself with

Pessimism is learned behavior, and spending too much time with people firmly embedded in a particular perspective can quickly rub off on you, too. Negativity is contagious, but so is happiness and well-being. As much as possible, seek out those who are happy, grounded, and deliberately resilient, and see what you can learn from the way they see things.

Tip 4: Be Stoical

Ancient Stoic philosophy emphasizes equanimity in the face of adversity that we cannot control—but first you have to be very clear about exactly what you can and cannot control. There really is no point in getting yourself worked up about something you cannot change. Such "counterfactual thinking" (for example, moaning about the weather, wishing things in the past were different, or "arguing against reality" in general) will only leave you feeling impotent and resentful.

Instead, save your energy for things you genuinely can influence in the world. The serenity prayer is a good reminder: "God, grant me the serenity to accept the things I cannot change, the courage to change the things I can, and the wisdom to know the difference."

Knowing when to push and when to let it go is a big part of optimism. You are never required to turn a blind eye or shrug your shoulders; rather, the skill comes in genuinely releasing the struggle against things that are not for you to decide.

To Master Your Feelings, Learn to Put Them into Words

We've already seen that we have a powerful symbolic way to interface with our physical brains: words. Knowing how to label and describe what we are feeling is an important first step in learning to manage, moderate, and regulate those feelings. Again, we return to the idea of acceptance and compassion. We can only label an experience if we are first willing to be present and accepting enough to acknowledge what that experience actually is!

Emotions are fundamentally ineffable, but we can use the medium of language to express them—not only to others but to ourselves. Once we know what we are experiencing and have a label for it, the experience somehow becomes smaller, more manageable, and less "fused" with us. Emotional literacy means understanding how we feel and knowing how to talk about it in a way that gives us control over what we do with those emotions. Very simply, if you don't know *what* you're feeling, you can't take control over feeling it.

"Affect Labeling" Increases Emotion Regulation

Putting words to your feelings can make them easier to deal with and can literally change the way your brain processes them. Translating what's going on in our inner world takes self-awareness, patience, and *discipline*.

A review paper by Torre and Liberman (2018) in the journal *Emotion* show how our emotional experiences can actually be changed by the labels we give them. Pausing long enough to consider the word for a feeling forces you to go into reappraisal mode—and this reappraisal alone makes feelings feel less intense. In one study, participants felt less emotional arousal when looking at negative pictures when they actively labeled their feelings, compared to when they didn't (Burklund et al. 2014).

This reduction in emotional arousal encompassed the whole body—heart rate, skin conductance, breathing, etc. Most interestingly, other studies using fMRIs have found that affect labeling decreases amygdala activity and increases activity in the ventrolateral prefrontal cortex (vlPFC)—the former is responsible for emotional processing, and the latter for regulating and controlling those emotions.

Torre and Lieberman proposed four potential ways that labeling brings about this result. The first is distraction, namely that labeling works simply because it interferes with our dwelling on the negative experience itself. After all, when we are labeling, we are not *feeling*.

Another possibility is that labeling affords an opportunity to self-reflect that would be impossible if we were still embroiled in the emotion itself. Emotional introspection has been shown to reduce activity in the amygdala even without labeling (Herwig et al. 2010).

A third possibility is that labeling reduces feelings of uncertainty, and this in turn lowers emotional arousal. This makes sense: When you are experiencing something but in a vague, nebulous sort of way, there is no real knowing what you are experiencing or how big it is. Putting a label on the feeling, however, immediately gives it a definite size and shape . . . and drives home the fact that it is limited. It is always less stressful and upsetting to "know what you're dealing with."

A final possibility is that labeling helps because it is a form of "symbolic conversion" where we use abstract thinking to gain psychological distance from an emotion. The feeling becomes words on a page or sounds on a tongue and somehow transformed into something less "real."

Whichever of these four possibilities is most likely (and it may be that labeling works for *all* these reasons), there is no doubt that putting your feelings into words gives you a certain advantage over them. Anything we can do to moderate a fight-or-flight reaction, lower stress, or bring about more calm and organization will help our brains.

One great side effect of building emotional literacy in this way is that it makes you a better communicator, which greatly improves your relationships. If you're in the middle of a hard conversation and feelings are running high, you may be tempted to shut down, run away, or go into attack mode and start laying blame. If you know how to pause, become self-aware, and give a name to the emotional processes underway, however, you instantly give yourself the chance to stand outside them . . . and thus control them.

When people are caught up in emotions, they stop thinking. They stop paying attention to their environments and they start reacting. If you can label emotions (yours or theirs), however, it's as though you can put a wedge into that spiral and stop it. It's as though you're saying, "Hey, do you notice what we're doing right now?"

When you can label your emotions, you can also own them, and this cuts down on a lot of confusion and hurt, especially in those difficult and overwrought conversations. For example, let's imagine someone witnesses you making a stupid mistake and you instantly react by lashing out at them and accusing them of getting in your way—maybe you even get angry and try to blame them for somehow causing the mistake. Soon, you're both having an angry argument about why the mistake was made and whose fault it really was.

If you can stop for a moment and become aware of your feelings, however, you might realize that you are not, in fact, angry at all. You're *embarrassed*. And the person who watched you make the mistake isn't feeling gleeful that you messed up; rather, they're offended that they're being blamed for nothing. If you can simply pause long enough to say, "I'm sorry I lost my temper. That was just really embarrassing for me," the entire conflict melts away.

When we are able to simply state how we feel ("*I* feel . . ."), then we are putting ourselves in the driver's seat of that emotion. We are not blaming anyone or putting the locus of control outside ourselves in any way. For example, being able to say, "I feel confused," offers you far, far more options for taking useful action in the world than incorrectly attributing your emotional state and saying things like, "This software is stupid," or, "Nobody designs things well anymore."

In this way, we can see the overlapping influence of the words we use, the filters we lay over reality, our interpretations, and our sense of optimism or pessimism over what we see. These things create our reality, and we have control over all of them.

This may all seem great in the abstract, but the challenge is to find a way to bring affective labeling into your everyday life when you most need it—i.e., all those times when emotions are running high. Here are some ways to practice getting a handle on things:

Stop. Take a Breath. Think.

The only way you can check in on what you're actually feeling is to stop and become conscious that you're feeling something in the first place. Every strong and seemingly uncontrollable emotion actually starts out as a small, manageable sensation. It can be difficult to slow down a speeding horse once it's escaped from the stable, but try to become aware of what's happening *before* that door is flung open and the horse bolts. That way, you give yourself the easier task of *avoiding* emotional overwhelm instead of the harder task of *managing* emotional overwhelm that's already started.

Just pause, take a breath, and talk to yourself internally for a moment. Ask, "What am I feeling right now?" Check in with your body. Then act from your self-awareness.

Put It Down in Black and White

As we've already seen, committing feelings to paper brings greater psychological distance, allowing you to defuse from the feeling and lower its intensity. From there, you can decide how to move forward with more self-control, poise, and conscious deliberation.

Open-ended journaling is great, but you can also lower your cognitive and emotional load by making lists, plans, and even mind maps to help you sort through your experience and begin to put shape to them. Remember that the brain is good at telling stories to make sense of its world. Putting words (and images) down is the first step to seeing what story is currently unfolding, as well as helping you begin to see alternative stories you could tell.

Speak It Out Loud

Another way to externalize and label any vague and amorphous inner feelings is to literally speak out loud what you're feeling—even if you're not quite sure what that is. Some people find it helpful to talk out loud to themselves, even imagining conversations between them and others, or between different parts of themselves.

Obviously, it's also useful if you can talk to someone real. Just be careful that you're not using your emotions to dominate, control, or manipulate others. It can be very powerful to just clearly and simply state how you feel, without any justification, explanation, or interpretation. "I think I'm feeling pretty discouraged right now." Then notice how it feels to own this emotion. Choose someone whom you can trust to simply listen, validate, and reflect that feeling.

Help Others Label Their Feelings

Whether you practice labeling your own feelings or the feelings of others, you are still cultivating the skill of emotional literacy. When you practice compassionate listening and affective labeling for others, you also strengthen your ability to do that for yourself. If you can accept and acknowledge other people's feelings with honesty and compassion, then you are also teaching yourself to take this attitude to your own emotions—even the ones that are messy, scary, or difficult to understand.

Remember not to make assumptions or judgments, and just let curiosity lead you. Use questions and respectful paraphrasing to gently put a name on people's experiences without trying to put words in their mouths.

"You sound like you're feeling a little defeated about it all. Is that right?"

It might not seem like changing the words and names for an experience could change the experience itself, but this is precisely what does happen. All you need to do is slow down for long enough to realize that you have this power, and you always have it, no matter how upset or overwhelmed you feel at any given moment.

Goal Setting Triggers Dopamine

We know that the brain likes to have a purpose and that it releases a cascade of feel-good hormones and neurotransmitters every time it achieves its purpose. After all, our understanding of reward and achievement comes first from our embodied experience of having reached an end we set for ourselves.

Many people like to say that dopamine is the reward molecule or the motivation neurotransmitter and so on, but this is not entirely true. It's the other way around—we feel the objective brain state of reward, pleasure, or motivation *because* of dopamine. This neurotransmitter is what tells our brain and body that something is worth pursuing. The way the body sends itself this message is to create almost addictive feelings of success, pleasure, achievement, and motivation.

Let's consider the process of goal setting from a purely neurobiological perspective and see exactly how the brain experiences and achieves goals. Neuroscientists are only scratching the surface on how the brain organizes its many parts, its eighty-six billion neurons, and the unspeakably huge number of possible connections between them. But what we do know is that **emotional investment** and **visualization** are both extremely important when it comes to setting and reaching goals.

Emotional investment means we are fully on board with a goal because, well, it feels good! Dopamine works in such a way that it almost tricks the brain into feeling as though it already has achieved the goal. Because we have an emotional investment in an outcome and feel like we can almost taste it, we are more motivated to move toward it. The amygdala is the emotional processing part of the brain, and this is the first part to be activated in the goal-setting process.

After you feel emotionally invested, however, it's time to make your visualized goal real, and that requires another part of your brain—the frontal lobe. This "higher" part of the brain is responsible for thinking through the details and plans of how you're actually going to achieve the emotionally satisfying end you've already visualized. It's as though the emotional drive is the fuel, and the visualization and planning are the ability to steer the vehicle in the right direction.

Now, dopamine is a neurotransmitter that's typically released *in anticipation of a reward.* It is motivating because it is released in reaction to us emotionally imagining and visualizing the end result—even if we haven't gotten there yet. Any time you're feeling productive, satisfied, motivated, and "in the zone," you can be certain that dopamine is pulling the strings and helping you feel wired up and focused on the goal. Serotonin plays a role, too, and is responsible for all those feelings of calm and contentment that are mixed in with the sense of a job well done—or rather, a job that will be well done very soon!

The Importance of Visualization

Social scientist and business consultant Dr. Frank Niles explained to Huffpost in his 2011 article "How to Use Visualization to Achieve Your Goals" that visualization goes far beyond superficial cliches like "if you can dream it, you can achieve it."

One crucial concept to understand is that your brain cannot actually discern the difference between *real* and *imagined*. For your brain, it's all just information and data. You can prove this to yourself by taking five minutes to imagine that you're biting into an extremely juicy and sour lemon and noticing that your body responds in exactly the same way it would if it were eating a real lemon—you salivate.

When you visualize, your neurons act "as if" what you're imagining is really true. Think about the profound implications of that! As you imagine, you create new neural pathways, and your dopamine and serotonin levels are there to help you *feel* the emotional reality of these new ideas, connections, and possibilities.

It's as though your brain does a "dress rehearsal" and lays down new neural connections, and then later decides how to make that new belief, expectation, or idea real. But to our brains, the goal is actually already real—and your plans and actions are simply there to bring the rest of reality into alignment.

A fascinating article in *Behavioral and Cognitive Neuroscience Reviews* (Compton 2003) explains it as follows:

> "First, emotional significance is evaluated pre-attentively by a subcortical circuit involving the amygdala; and second, stimuli deemed emotionally significant are given priority in the competition for access to selective attention. This process involves bottom-up inputs from the amygdala as well as top-down influences from frontal lobe regions involved in goal setting and maintaining representations in working memory. The review highlights limitations in the current literature, directions for fruitful future research, and the need to move beyond simple dichotomies such as 'cognition' versus 'emotion.'"

To simplify—the amygdala is the first to evaluate the importance and significance of a goal, and it does this via emotion. The frontal lobe works out the specifics. The two are not really distinct, however; rather they work together like two sides of the same coin, guiding your focus onto what matters and helping you ignore everything that's not relevant to your goal.

So, emotional investment is absolutely essential for goal setting and a big part of the mechanism for how your brain starts to make changes in the world. This means that we cannot bypass the emotional (read, neurochemical) part of the process—rather this should be our first step. Once you've got a hold of the feeling of the goal you want to achieve (and meaning and purpose will definitely play a role in how good something feels), then you can begin to take the next steps.

Make Your Goals Realistic—But Challenging

The sense of reward is proportionate to the size of the challenge and the adversity overcome. The trick is to choose a goal that is genuinely within your grasp, but not one that is so impossible that it will demoralize you.

Yes, SMART Goals Matter

The old advice holds true—set goals that are *specific, measurable, achievable, relevant, and time bound*. Don't assume that emotional investment alone is enough—you need to have a clear, detailed understanding of exactly what you're trying to do so that you can easily tell when you've achieved it.

Avoid setting goals that are vague or unclear, goals that can't be tracked in any way, goals that are not possible, goals that don't make sense for you, and goals that have no fixed deadline, i.e., "one day" goals.

Break It Down

The process of achieving your goals is a complex back-and-forth interplay between seeing the grand finale in your mind's eye, but also zooming in to the present so you can look at all the small, practical steps that take you, bit by bit, to that goal.

Breaking down goals into smaller steps is a great way to manage overwhelm and lower anxiety, but it also gives you a clear game plan for exactly how to get from A to B. What's more, a series of smaller goals gives you the opportunity to experience a mini reward every time you reach that new milestone. Each time, your brain gets a little dopamine hit, which sends the chemical message, "That's amazing! That feels so good! You're on the right track. Keep going and maybe there will be another great feeling just around the corner!"

Goals that are too big can lead to feelings of intimidation, which fuel procrastination and avoidance. Instead, work with your brain to almost "gamify" the process, and set up plenty of opportunities for reward and celebration along the way. If things are still feeling tough, just break tasks down even further.

Tap into Your Bigger Purpose

While the Compton paper showed how the amygdala and frontal lobe work in concert to achieve a goal, there is another aspect to the process. Your brain possesses the quality of neuroplasticity, which means that it can change according to the functions it is asked to serve. This means that making goals quite literally changes your brain and makes it better optimized to achieve that goal.

A study at the University of Texas found that multiple sclerosis patients who set ambitious goals actually had fewer symptoms than those who didn't (Alexa et al. 2003). Another study showed that when goals are emotional (that is, people felt emotionally motivated and connected to the goal), people were more likely to see the goal as less difficult (Cole et al. 2013).

Remember the Nietzsche quote that said that "man can endure any how if he has a why"? Well, this research strongly suggests that this is true—having an emotionally resonating *why* may change your brain's perception so that the challenge in front of it starts to look far more manageable.

Summary:

- Optimism is a good brain habit that you can use discipline to consciously cultivate for yourself. Optimism is both a personality trait and a product of our environment, and we have some scope to deliberately cultivate it. Optimism is an active, constructive state of mind that goes beyond mere positivity.
- Optimists interpret their perceptions of the world in the way that best allows them to cope. It's the state of mind that acknowledges a person's power to act, choose, and solve problems.
- Knowing how to label and describe what we are feeling is an important first step in learning to manage, moderate, and regulate those feelings. Master your feelings with affect labeling. Emotional literacy means understanding how we feel, giving us the choice of what we do with those emotions. Labeling feelings can make them easier to deal with and literally change the way the brain processes them.
- Goal setting triggers the release of dopamine and activates the brain's reward system. Emotional investment and visualization are both important

when it comes to setting and reaching goals. Once you are emotionally invested (amygdala), you visualize your goal and take concrete steps toward making it real (frontal lobe).
- Visualization creates new neural pathways. Your brain cannot tell the difference between *real* and *imagined*. The amygdala evaluates the importance of a goal via emotion, and then the frontal lobe works out the details.

Chapter 6: The Agile Brain

When we consider the neuroscience of the brain in terms of what the brain's functions are, then we see that, as an organ, the brain has evolved for all the many complex survival tasks demanded of a human being: keeping healthy and safe, connecting harmoniously with the tribe, using symbols and language to make sense of the world, plugging into sources of meaning, purpose, and direction, and staying strong and determined in the face of challenge, uncertainty, and adversity.

So far, so good. In this final chapter, we will look at one more important function of a happy brain: adaptation. Part of what makes human beings the unique organisms they are is that they can respond and react to unknowns in the environment. The human brain is capable of imagining the future, planning for it, and anticipating and avoiding potential danger. Every creature has evolved and adapted to thrive in its unique environmental milieu, but what makes humans special is that they are able to encounter unexpected novelty in the world and adapt very quickly to it.

Our ability to engage with novelty goes beyond just surviving it—instead we use the potential of newness and the unexpected to help us be more creative, solve problems, and use curiosity to drive our hunger to learn more about the world. In other words, the brain was built for *novelty*.

The Spice of Life

Most of us can remember the particularly dull, mindless feeling that fell over everything during the months of lockdown over the pandemic. Stuck at home, people's worlds shrank, there wasn't much newness to stimulate the brain, and every day brought the same tedium and predictability as the day before it. People actually noticed subtle signs of cognitive decline: poorer memories, worse mood, and a rapid decline in social and communication skills.

Dr. Laurie Santos is a cognitive scientist and Yale lecturer and puts it succinctly: "There is a connection between novelty and happiness.

Novel stimuli tend to activate regions of our brain that are associated with rewards." Yup, it's our friend dopamine again!

Newness in your environment is often felt by the brain to be intrinsically rewarding and has far-reaching influences on your attention, brain connectivity, and mood. A fun study asked its participants to move around New York City and Miami as the researchers tracked their GPS data and monitored their daily moods. The team lead Dr. Aaron Heller said this of the data gathered:

> "What we found was that for every person, on days when they displayed greater exploration, greater "roaming entropy," they reported feeling happier. It's as simple as that. [. . .] The experience of novelty, or going to places you had never been before, actually seemed to have an even larger association with positive emotion on that day" (Heller et al. 2020).

The relationship is bidirectional, however: If you explore more, you feel better, and the better you feel, the more inclined you are to keep exploring.

Novelty has been said to make us more resilient, more curious, and happier overall.

The more we actively engage with our environment, the more alive and connected we feel, and the more we discover opportunities to create rewarding situations, bond with others, and learn or demonstrate our own mastery (i.e., boost our self-esteem).

You don't have to live in New York City in order to have a novel and exciting life, though—you don't even have to "explore" in the conventional sense. Rather, novelty is a way of being that prioritizes all new and unknown things in every area of life. Changes and unexpected variations don't have to be big to pique your brain's interest and get you engaged again.

Tali Sharot is a cognitive neuroscience professor at University College London, and she writes about what's called habituation. Simply, when the neurons in the brain become habituated, it means they have become fatigued with certain unchanging stimuli of everyday life. This phenomenon is not reserved for the brain and can be applied to all sorts of sensory overstimulation. For example, if you jump into a cold pool, the temperature sensation will be thrilling and very much the focus of your attention. But after ten minutes, your body acclimatizes to the temperature and you no longer register it as novel. Indeed, if you stayed in the pool long enough, you'd eventually get bored of that specific stimulus.

This is an important observation because it tells us that the objective measure of the value of an experience is irrelevant when it comes to its *novelty* power. A change—any change—can stimulate the brain, and it doesn't matter if the new stimulus is objectively better than the old stimulus. In the same vein, even wonderful stimuli lose their shine after a while, and even the most ideal and enjoyable daily routine will grow tiresome if it never changes.

There can be such a thing as too much novelty, which can lead to information overload and the perception that novelty and uncertainty are threatening rather than exciting. A healthy, stimulated life falls somewhere in between the two extremes.

How do you build more novelty into your life? Think of the excitement for novelty as a side effect of our brain's inbuilt mechanisms for learning and adaptation. Your brain *wants* to learn—so give it plenty of new things to experience!

- Go somewhere new or take a new route to a familiar place
- Eat new foods or try new restaurants

- Meet new people
- Wear new clothes, or old clothes in new ways
- Change your hairstyle
- Take up a new hobby
- Read a new book you wouldn't otherwise read
- Try a new activity
- Do all the things you normally do—but at different times of day or in different ways (or with different people, for that matter)
- Experiment with new ideas, opinions, and beliefs

The substantia nigra/ventral segmental area in the brain (or SN/VTA for short) is known as the "novelty center," and activity here is closely connected with the amygdala and hippocampus—the big emotion processors. These parts of the brain respond to novel incoming stimuli and compare them against existing memories. The amygdala then formulates an emotional reaction given these long-term associations and memories.

In a 2006 paper called *Pure Novelty Spurs the Brain*, Bunzeck and Düzel explained the results of their "oddball experiment." Study participants were shown images of boring everyday items (faces, doors, etc.), and occasionally an "oddball" image was thrown in—which immediately activated the SN/VTA. New information stands out. It makes our brains pay attention. The experiment only worked, however, when participants saw an image *they had never seen before*—i.e., it had to be genuinely novel.

Curiously, dopamine pathways were also activated on seeing these unexpected images. The authors suggested that novelty may have an important relationship with motivation and our desire to seek out rewards. Basically, the brain reacts to novelty by releasing dopamine—which then spurs us to get out there and explore this new aspect of the environment.

If you are battling low enthusiasm and procrastination, you may find that you feel a boost of motivation when the task is suddenly switched up or something fun and unexpected happens. Novelty is exciting because there is a vague promise of reward in it. Think about a magical fairy door in front of you that says Open Me on the front. It's novel and unknown. But immediately you are motivated to open that door—you wouldn't think of putting it off to do later. Why? Well, there may be something wonderful behind that door. The sense of awe and enchantment we feel when faced with such novelty may really be the experience of having dopamine course through our brains!

Dr. Düzel explains, "The brain learns that the stimulus, once familiar, has no reward associated with it, and so it loses its potential. For this reason, only completely new objects activate the midbrain area and increase our levels of dopamine." We may lose motivation for an old task simply because we already know that there is nothing new to be gained from it. It's like playing a video game where all the tokens have already been gathered and the challenges completed. Now you can see why it's so essential to break tasks down and reward yourself for each one!

Dr. David Eagleman is another well-known neuroscientist who emphasizes the value of novelty in stimulating the brain, improving memory, and promoting resilience and social well-being. His advice for adding more of the "spice of life" is pretty common sense:

- Make small, everyday changes and experience something new frequently, rather than trying to cram loads of novelty into a single big event, like a vacation (although vacations are great, too!).

- Keep doing what you do, but find creative ways to add a twist. You don't have to spend any extra money or time—just get curious about life outside your rut.

- Take a break from the normal day-to-day routine, even if it's a healthy, balanced routine. Your favorite activities will still be there waiting for you if you go off and explore something else for a while.

- Think about a range of first-time experiences you've never had and see what you can do to try them out here and now. Have you always wanted to try Norwegian food, do an improv class, or ride a camel? Now's the time.

Creativity and Brain Health

The brain is not just able to perceive, enjoy, and adapt to novelty in its environment—it's also able to generate that novelty itself. In other words, the human brain can be creative. In much the same way as novelty releases the reward-inducing dopamine, so, too, does creativity, with some research showing that certain forms of creative expression activate the reward pathways and lead to measurable feelings of pleasure.

In a 2017 study in the journal *The Arts in Psychotherapy*, Kaimal et al. found increased blood flow to the brain's various reward centers whenever study participants were asked to partake in a "visual expression exercise" such as doodling, sketching, or coloring.

The finding implies that there are concrete positive brain states associated with art and the act of creation. The study's authors suggest this may have important implications for treating mood disorders and regulating disturbed reward circuitry. In the context of what we know about the brain-boosting power of novelty, storytelling, affect labeling, meaning and purpose, stress relief, and even socializing (if art is done with other people), it's easy to see how a creative hobby can act as a powerful sustainer of mental well-being.

Another 2016 study published in the *Journal of the American Art Therapy Association* showed that just forty-five minutes of artmaking in a studio setting significantly lowered cortisol levels in study participants. Interestingly, the kind of art produced made no difference, and neither did the training, talent, or skill level of the people involved. This suggests that the value of creating art is not in the final work produced, but rather in the process of creation itself.

Any artist can confirm that the creative process can often be transcendent. Artmaking can occasionally produce deep flow states, total immersion, and extreme focus, especially when expressing something personally meaningful. A 2018 study in *Frontiers of Psychology* measured increased alpha wave activity all throughout the brain during the creative process, but also noted activation in those networks connected to relaxation, focus, and enjoyment.

Making Art Is a Healthy Brain Habit

Do you think that you're a "creative person"?

What if *everyone* is a creative person, and creativity is as natural to every human being as dreaming or speaking?

Many of us have quietly decided that art and creativity are not for us, but when you think about it, this attitude is pretty bizarre. We imagine that we are not permitted to express ourselves creatively unless our work is 100 percent novel, commercially viable, or of an extremely high standard (what does that mean, anyway?).

But you can shift this attitude and see creativity as more of an expression of your personal perspective, your perception, your unique you-ness. The way that you see the world, the words you use to describe it, and the distinctive style you put on your interpretation of what's around you . . . *that's* creativity.

Art, originality, and imagination are all around us. Every time you connect two ideas together, you're being creative. Every time you look at something familiar in a strange way, you're being creative, too. In a sense, creativity can be thought of as a blend of play, exploration, and language—you are interacting with reality in your own unique way and communicating the results. Not only is it a process that's rewarding in its own right, but it also turns out that this kind of expressive play is extremely healthy for your brain.

In the 1926 classic book *The Art of Thought*, Graham Wallas, social psychologist and co-founder of the London School of Economics, outlined a four-part model of the creative process:

> "The first in time I shall call **Preparation**, the stage during

which the problem was 'investigated... in all directions'; the second is the stage during which he was not consciously thinking about the problem, which I shall call **Incubation**; the third, consisting of the appearance of the 'happy idea' together with the psychological events which immediately preceded and accompanied that appearance, I shall call **Illumination**. And I shall add a fourth stage, of **Verification**..."

During preparation we make plans and use past work and previous experience to start examining the problem or potential idea. During incubation we hold off from taking any conscious action and let our unconscious mind process the possibilities. The third stage can be quite exciting—illumination is where the muses strike, the art comes into being, and something clicks into place. The "psychological events" flow directly from the previous two stages of preparation and incubation.

Finally, the verification stage is where we check and appraise what has been created. Just because something has come via flash of insight or creative energy, it doesn't mean it's fully formed! The verification process is where we come out of our emotional, amygdala-focused brain state and enter into a more conscious, deliberate, and slower frontal lobe mode.

As you can see, Wallas's model contains room for many of the neurological processes we've already discovered. These include rest, wherein the brain can consolidate and recuperate (incubation), emotional and meaningful visualization of the end goal (preparation), storytelling, variety and optimism (illumination), and the more disciplined, focused states of deep work (verification).

The creative process, then, is both the result of and the cause of a healthy, vibrant brain working to its fullest purpose and potential. It's not a single event, but a synchronized *process* that involves many different parts of the brain over time. Creative people are not just those who have mastered whimsy or originality, but the whole suit of skills that capture an unexpected "*aha* moment" and consciously bring it shape and form. "Convergent" thinking is the process of whittling things down to fundamental principles, finding similarities and connections between disparate ideas, and concretizing. "Divergent" thinking, on the other hand, goes in the other direction and expands on a single idea to create many more. To illustrate the difference:

Convergent thinking: You consider the idea of a cow, a sheep, and a goat, and your brain tells you that the single thing unifying these is the category "four-legged farm animals." You have converged three into one.

Divergent thinking: You look at these four-legged farm animals and challenge yourself to create as many new fantasy animals as you can from your imagination. You create the "runk," which has long, silky white fur, and the "drebbit," which is like a four-legged ostrich, only it has big ears, and so on. Theoretically, you could dream up an infinite number of new animals from the single prompt "four-legged farm animals" and so diverge from this single point.

Both types of thinking are required during the creative process in just the same way as *both* rest and deep work are required to be productive and effective. The brain doesn't really have a "creative center." Rather, it's about the coordinated and synchronized use of the frontal lobe, the hippocampus, the basal ganglia, the amygdala, and all the many millions of neural connections in the white matter. Just like creativity itself, what matters is *how you use* the materials at hand.

So, how do we become more creative? How do we use our knowledge about the creative process to improve our brain health?

Tip 1: Intentionally create "bad art"

One of the biggest impediments to creativity is the faulty belief that we are not allowed to make mistakes or produce something "bad." The irony is that most of the time, in order to produce something great, an artist often has to first produce vast amounts of art that's not so great!

Detach from judging the end product and instead just become curious about how it feels to make new things. Make your goal to simply produce no matter what. Many authors repeat the adage, "take care of the quantity and the quality will take care of itself."

Take it further and detach from the quality of the outcome entirely. You can do this by not showing other people your work at first and taking care not to prejudge your creations before you've even made them (because, in many cases, you are your worst and most critical judge!). Reframe your exercise as mere play. Decide to create bad art on purpose so you are free from the inhibition that comes from thinking, "I can't mess this up." Yes, you can! You can mess it up *a lot* and it makes no difference!

This attitude will keep you firmly in the first three stages of Wallas's process—and keep your meddling, "editing," and verifying mind away while you simply enjoy creating.

Tip 2: "Only connect"

In a way, there is no real possibility of creating something new from nothing, unless you're God. But what we do have endless liberty to do is combine what already exists in endlessly novel and unexpected ways. If you think about noteworthy works of art, whether that's painting, music, novels, or something else, you'll see that the artists responsible used pre-existing material, only in a way that had not quite been done before.

Bearing in mind the thrilling effect that novelty has on the brain, consciously choose to create your own original combinations and connections. You can practice this "skill" all throughout the day, based on literally any stimulus you come across. For example, if you're at the store buying groceries, play a game where you imagine a crazy dish you could make using *all* the things you've put in the cart so far, or imagine that the place is suddenly overrun with zombies—how would you use these items to survive or defend yourself?

Tip 3: Embrace constraints

Remember that creativity is *not* just about wild, free-form expansion and divergent thinking. In fact, most people find they are more creative when they are operating within a narrower set of constraints. If someone asked you to "write something outlandish," you may suddenly find yourself with writer's block. But what if they asked you to "write a short story of just five hundred words from a dog's point of view as it describes its owner's workday to a bulldog it meets at the park"?

Sometimes, the brain is more generative in the face of lack or absence. It takes real creativity to write a poem without using the letter e, for example, or create a picture without using any straight lines at all. There is ultimately a big overlap between creativity and problem-solving—the same parts of your brain are asking, "How can I get around this little obstacle? What new way forward haven't I imagined yet?" Overcoming such obstacles also provides a greater dopamine hit and sense of reward, meaning, and achievement.

So, rather than removing all limits and telling yourself the sky is the limit, embrace constraints, obstacles, restrictions, and boundaries because these are the secret wellspring of creativity.

How to be more creative in everyday life is itself a creative endeavor—what should you try? Well, that's up to you! Enroll in a pottery or creative writing class, or simply go to the craft store with no plan in mind and see what happens. Scribble and doodle, mix up your language, rearrange the furniture, deliberately choose not to follow the recipe, or put together a new or unusual outfit.

Mindset: Think Growth, Create Growth

In her now well-regarded best-selling 2007 book *Mindset*, psychologist Carol Dweck explains how our perceptions, expectations, and beliefs (i.e., mindset) ultimately influence our experience, our actions, and how well we are able to thrive in life. In fact, when it comes to success in life, she sees the presence of a "growth mindset" as more important than any innate talent or intelligence.

In particular, Dweck is interested in how profoundly we are influenced by our own thoughts about talent and ability—rather than our talent and ability per se. Dweck explains that a fixed mindset is one that sees intelligence and ability as, well, *fixed* quantities. In other words, you are born with an ability or you aren't, and if you aren't, then there is no real way to acquire it (so don't bother).

On the other hand, there is the growth mindset, which is the perspective that growth and development are possible, and that things like intelligence and talent are actually not set traits but more like habits to be acquired. It's this attitude, Dweck argues, that most reliably predicts success. As she says, "It's not always the people who start out the smartest who end up the smartest."

With a fixed mindset, you set your life on a path of self-fulfilling prophesies. Let's say you don't achieve in school and so you conclude that you are unintelligent by nature. Because of your belief that you cannot possibly change this innate limitation, you unconsciously select jobs that do not challenge you, and find yourself in situations that confirm your limitations rather than stimulate your potential. In time, your actions actually confirm your original conclusion that you are just a natural-born underachiever.

You may already be familiar with Dweck's theory, but there is now plenty of interesting research to suggest that "mindset" is not some vague, abstract quality but rather also a "brainset" and something that we can literally see unfolding in the brain itself.

In the above example of the underachiever, the habitual beliefs, expectations, and assumptions about the world are actually engraved into the brain's neural circuitry, and the more those thoughts are thought, the easier it is to keep on thinking them. So, the brain starts out by interpreting the world . . . but if that interpretation is held long enough, actions are taken in line with it, and in time the world starts to actually resemble the assumptions made about it. The brain is shaped by reality. But it shapes reality in turn.

It would be wrong to think that only underachievers have a fixed mindset, however. The "paradox of expertise" tells us that even successful people can get trapped in their idea of being "finished" and somehow not requiring any further development. This is why we encounter so-called experts who nevertheless make errors that a layperson never would. Repeatedly failing to recognize learning opportunities (because remember, the fixed mindset tells you that there fundamentally *is* no real way to learn) has an obvious consequence: failing to learn.

Salman Khan of the Khan Academy recommends that teachers and parents praise children's ability to grow, and not just their innate, fixed intelligence. There is a big difference between "Wow, look how hard you've worked and how well you did" and "Look how clever you are."

In the latter case, if the child should suddenly find themselves struggling, they might conclude that this means they are at the limit of their intelligence or weren't intelligent to start off with. The only way out is to give up (after being humiliated that you "failed").

The child who is praised for their *effort*, however, may develop a growth mindset, and when they fail, they may think, "Oh, this is tough, but that's okay. I just need to work harder to figure it out." At the end of the day, the one who works hard has the greater likelihood of succeeding, even if they originally were not especially talented or intelligent.

The growth mindset, then, is the very thing that permits literal growth in the brain—the development and expansion of new neural pathways. Believing that growth is possible makes it possible. Believing that you are what you are and can never change acts as a self-fulfilling prophesy, shrinking your mental horizons . . . and your literal brain.

Your Brain Is Fantastically Neuroplastic

Your brain is a tool that changes shape depending on the task it needs to perform. If you give it no task, it atrophies and gets good at doing nothing. If you give it the same task over and over, it gets good at doing that task. If you give it many tasks to do, however, and you constantly challenge and stimulate it, it adapts by becoming as flexible as possible. If you constantly train your brain to grow, learn, and evolve, then *that* is what it will become good at. Train it to look for data it already "knows" is true, and it will just as dutifully perform that task, ignoring everything else.

The neural pathways our brain follows represent the perspectives, habits, interpretations, beliefs, and actions that we routinely return to. If the brain can learn a habit, however, then it can unlearn it—and learn a new one. Ironically, the first step to adopting a healthier growth mindset is to recognize the possibility of doing so in the first place. Even if your mindset is squarely fixed right now, that doesn't mean that you have to be that way forever.

With a growth mindset, your brain is:

- More flexible, adaptable, and neuroplastic.
- Better able to cultivate and take advantage of the dopamine released by small wins and learning experiences, increasing motivation (Ng 2018).

- Able to dampen the fear response, identify and learn from mistakes, and reduce stress in the face of setbacks (Moser et al. 2011).
- Better able to learn and remember and sustain attention, especially regarding mistakes and how they can be improved on (Schroder et al. 2017).
- Better primed to solve problems and spot opportunities, improve when given feedback, and develop "grit" (Myers et al. 2016).

Curiosity—such as the curiosity that prompted you to read this book—is an amazing first step. Merely exposing yourself to new stimuli (there's novelty and creativity again!) stimulates the brain to think new thoughts. The good news is that your brain wants to be in learning mode. It's really just habit, fear, and laziness that get in the way. Here are some ways to shake things up:

Listen for the Voice of the Fixed Mindset—and Challenge It

A fixed mindset is expressed as automatic negative self-talk that tries to convince you that growth is simply not possible. For example:

"You're no good at XYZ. It's just not your thing."

"Those other people find it easy. If you find it hard, that's the proof that you're not cut out for this!"

"You don't know how to do this now, so that means you'll never know."

"If you fail, everyone will see how stupid/talentless/incapable you are."

Try to reframe these assumptions—although it may feel unnatural at first. When you catch yourself speaking from the assumption that you are what you are and can never change, gently challenge yourself and try to replace the thought with something that recognizes your ability to learn and adapt:

"You don't know how to do this . . . yet. What first step can you take to learning more?"

"Learning is tough sometimes. Expect difficulties along the way, but that's part of the process!"

"The more you practice, the easier this gets."

"Failing is not an issue — doing things 'wrong' helps you understand how to do them right. You're still a worthwhile and valuable person even if it takes you time to get things right."

Own Your Right to Choose

With a fixed mindset, it can sometimes feel like the success of your life is largely out of your hands. It rests with whatever traits you were born with, and this in turn seems to come down to luck, genetics, or fate—but not to you. This is called having an external locus of control, and it can be extremely disempowering.

To start gently undoing this belief, notice how often you are actually given the choice as to how you want to act. For example, rather than automatically assuming that something isn't "for you" or that you are too old/stupid/whatever to try something new, realize that you are actually being presented with a choice to make. You can *choose* to try. You are not doomed to carry on in the same way you always have.

Having a growth mindset doesn't mean that you wholeheartedly throw yourself into learning every new thing under the sun. While mindset matters, there are of course some natural limitations that we all possess. And realistically, there just isn't enough time to pursue everything we set our heart on!

That said, we can legitimately turn down new possibilities to learn and new avenues to explore because we *choose* to. Compare "I suck at math and will never learn" with "I don't really enjoy math and don't need to know much of it, given my goals. But if it ever becomes necessary, I trust that I can figure it out."

Make Friends with Failure

One of the most obvious places you will spot evidence of a fixed mindset is in the wake of failure. Indeed, we can see the whole idea of failure itself as a fixed mindset phenomenon. In the growth mindset, there really isn't such a thing as failure—there is just the long and windy path necessary to take in order to arrive at mastery (which, by the way, you never really reach!).

A fixed mindset easily sees its "traits" (intelligence, talent) as innate and therefore a part of the character and very identity of a person. That means that a person who fails doesn't just fail but *becomes a failure.* A fixed mindset, then, makes one simultaneously more egotistical, less resilient, and more vulnerable to adversity. In order to avoid the humiliation of failing (i.e., an attack on your very identity), you avoid taking on any challenges that you can't be sure of winning, or you get embarrassed and demoralized when you do fail, and either give up or resort to blame or excuses.

The growth mindset sees failure as part of the learning process. That's all. There is no ego in it. Every outcome is valuable because it represents one more step on the journey to figuring things out. While a fixed mindset might have you beating yourself up for not doing better, and wanting to run away and stick to things you already know and understand, the growth mindset asks, "Why didn't I do well? What should I have done instead? This is interesting. What does it teach me? I didn't do that right . . . but what *did* I do right and how can I keep doing more of that?"

The biggest difference between a growth mindset and a fixed mindset is not about mindset at all, but about *action*. A growth mindset is constantly asking questions, trying things out, testing and adjusting hypotheses, and taking concrete action in the world in order to learn in a hands-on way.

For the Brain, Curiosity Equals Reward

An agile brain is one that is plastic. It can change, adapt, grow, learn, and adjust itself according to feedback from its environment. Not only does change not threaten the healthy brain, but it actually stimulates and strengthens it, causing it to thrive and expand in capability.

As we've hinted at throughout this book, a key characteristic behind this open-ended and receptive state of mind is curiosity. We will end the chapter and the book on a quality that is perhaps most fundamental to all the other aspects considered so far. Without curiosity, none of the brain's other capacities—creativity, problem-solving, connecting to others, storytelling, reflecting, seeking purpose, learning—ever get off the ground. Curiosity is always the start.

From the moment a baby is born, it is in sudden and direct relationship with the environment, and the brain is the tool that helps it optimize this connection. Have you ever seen a labrador puppy as it bounds into a room it's never been in before? It shoots in with purpose and energy, tail wagging, nose going everywhere to sniff everything, greeting everyone. Everything in its perception, behavior, and attitude seems to say, "What's here for me?!"

A healthy brain is pretty much like that labrador puppy. It enters into the world with a lively, irrepressible curiosity and wants to know and get into *everything*!

The drive to seek out new information, to make use of it, to understand, to participate, and to extract fun and meaning and value—these things don't just belong to labrador puppies, but to human beings. Life may have taught us to dampen our expectations, to expect the worst, or to stop asking questions. If we can reconnect with this innate sense of curiosity in ourselves, however, we may find that it never really went away.

The curiosity brain state comes with heightened activity in those areas associated with learning and memory. The dopamine system is activated, and we feel rewarded and motivated to keep finding out more. The old saying goes that curiosity killed the cat . . . but the rest of the saying is that "satisfaction brought it back"!

Research findings from Ranganath and colleagues (2014; 2019) suggest that curiosity triggers changes in the brain that prepare us to learn, pay attention, and remember. In one study, researchers instructed participants to review a series of questions and say how curious they felt to learn the answer. They then examined their brains using fMRI as they re-exposed them to the questions they rated as most curiosity-inducing.

After a few follow-up tests, the researchers found that the higher the curiosity created for a particular question, the better the memory for the answer to that question. In fact, this boost in memory even seemed to influence unrelated stimuli, since participants were also better able to remember a photograph of a face if they had first seen a question that they subjectively rated as curiosity-provoking.

What can we make of these results? When the brain is in a curious state, it is actively seeking information—and this active information-seeking focuses the attention and seemingly improves memory formation and retrieval. On closer inspection, researchers found that curiosity correlated with increased activity in the ventral tegmental area and nucleus accumbens—regions of the brain known to transmit and regulate dopamine, which we know modulates feelings of reward and motivation.

In other words, the researchers found a brain state analogous to "eager interest" or "anticipation," and this sense of dopamine-modulated reward was precisely what sharpened the brain's learning ability. Just like the labrador puppy who is wondering what fantastic thing it will find in a new room, your curious brain is experiencing heightened attention and anticipation for some kind of informational reward.

Curious minds learn more. Ranganath believes that understanding these mechanisms holds interesting implications for those with learning difficulties, especially where disturbance to the dopamine system is a feature—such as with Parkinson's disease. But even in the absence of a learning issue, such research strongly suggests that if we wish to learn well, we need to consciously activate our sense of curiosity and enlist our brain's natural reward system. Some theorists believe that this is precisely the reason these systems evolved in the first place!

Four Kinds of Curiosity

Daniel Berlyne is a British-Canadian experimental and theoretical psychologist who has worked extensively in the field of curiosity and how it links to arousal, conflict, novelty, and uncertainty. Berlyne's idea is that moderately complex and ambiguous stimuli create an optimal state of arousal in the human brain, and this arousal compels people to seek a resolution.

Berlyne identified two axes along which attention and arousal fall, which creates a matrix of four different types of curiosity, as shown below (Travis [2024], inspired by Berlyne [1960] and Loewenstein [1994]; figure based on Anderson [2013]). On one axis we can see a continuum between perceptual versus epistemic, and on the other, the continuum between diversive and specific.

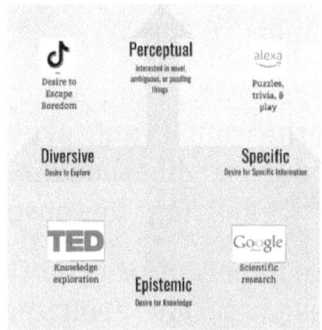

Epistemic curiosity is all about what you know. It involves systematically finding ways to fill your own knowledge gaps and absorb new information, usually by experiment, research, and questioning. It's about ideas and facts. Interestingly, when people talk about a "thirst" or a "hunger" for knowledge, this may not be a metaphor—epistemic curiosity seems to trigger brain activity not unlike the response to bodily hunger or thirst. Furthermore, the satisfaction of the hunger and thirst for knowledge releases a rewarding shot of dopamine, just as it does when we literally eat or drink.

To cultivate this form of knowledge, you may read, research, or debate with knowledgeable others.

Perceptual curiosity is more about data coming in from your sense organs—i.e., the world as you can see, smell, touch, hear, and taste it. This is the more embodied form of engaging with new stimuli.

Cultivating this form of curiosity requires only that you explore the world around you! Take a new route through your neighborhood or spend an hour in a forest, following your nose.

Both epistemic and perceptual curiosity work together. You may be deeply curious about the amazing aromas of an unknown dish you encounter in a restaurant (perceptual curiosity), but once you've eaten it, you may start to wonder what it's called, where it comes from, how the dish is made, etc. (epistemic curiosity).

Specific curiosity is focused and targeted around a particular question. This is the curiosity that comes from, for example, not knowing the missing letters in Wheel of Fortune or of wondering who the murderer in a murder mystery is (this mirrors the convergent thinking we discussed earlier).

Diversive curiosity is a broader interest in the world in general, with no specific goal beyond learning something, *anything*, new. It's a little like walking into a museum just to see what you can see.

Though there are four distinct types of curiosity shown in the graph above, in reality the different types overlap, and one type may flow into another. Certain curiosity modes may be more useful for particular problems or situations, and there may be individual preferences for the default curiosity mode in different people.

There is arguably another form of curiosity, called empathic curiosity, which is an interest in other people's thoughts and feelings. Naturally, this kind of inquisitiveness is especially useful for deeper and more meaningful social connections, but it can also interact with the other forms of curiosity. For example, one form of curiosity may lead you to seek out and build a relationship with someone you find fascinating, while another form will have you approaching people's emotions in general as an academic question (much like Berlyne himself!).

What can we do with all this information?

One possibility is to take stock of your current daily routines and ask yourself whether you might need a little more curiosity (and satisfaction) to stimulate your brain. You may find that you tend to prefer one form of curiosity over another—but what about the other types, and how might you introduce them?

The thing about curiosity is that it cannot really be faked. There is no point in pursuing things just because they seem like they *should* be interesting. Either they are or they aren't! Don't worry if your interests seem weird or your questions seem foolish. If something is sparking your curiosity, follow it down the rabbit hole and see where it goes.

Many of us have busy lives that we fill with obligations and, when we get the time, rest and recreation. Life can quickly become dull, however, if nothing around you seems worth your deeper attention and investigation.

Ask questions. Some people like to keep a journal where they jot down everything that pops into their minds. There are probably dozens of things you wonder about everyday. Don't let that curiosity go by, but rather seize it and investigate further. The great thing about curious questions is that they tend to generate more and more curious questions. Stay open-minded, have a growth mindset, and keep following that little spark of fascination.

Your brain will become more alert and engaged, you'll feel great, and you may just learn something. Your world gets bigger. The irony is that people who have lost curiosity feel as though they live in a boring world they already know everything about. Curious people, however, seem to discover infinite new adventures, mysteries, and attractions everywhere they look.

Summary:

- One function of a happy brain is to learn, adapt, and grow—for this it needs agility and flexibility. The brain was built for novelty, which activates regions of the brain associated with rewards.
- Novelty may have an important relationship with motivation and our desire to seek out rewards since it triggers dopamine release. To introduce novelty, find ways to expose yourself to new experiences and situations.
- Creative expression activates the brain's reward pathways, lowers stress, and boosts well-being. Boost brain health by cultivating a regular art habit, even if you don't consider yourself creative. Art follows the stages of preparation, incubation, illumination, and verification; we use all parts of our brains during the creative process.

- Intentionally create bad art, play around with connection-making, and embrace constraints to spur creativity.
- Our mindset influences our experience; our actions; how well we are able to adapt, learn, and thrive; and our total brain health. A fixed mindset sees intelligence and ability as innate and fixed, whereas a growth mindset sees learning as possible. A growth mindset is correlated with greater brain health and function. The growth mindset permits brain growth and the development and expansion of new neural pathways.
- Encourage neuroplasticity by asking questions, staying curious, and embracing failure as the path to mastery and learning. Curious minds learn more.

www.ingramcontent.com/pod-product-compliance
Lightning Source LLC
Chambersburg PA
CBHW060605080526
44585CB00013B/685